The Critical Media Literacy Guide

Brill Guides to Scholarship in Education

The titles published in this series are listed at *brill.com/bgse*

The Critical Media Literacy Guide

Engaging Media and Transforming Education

By

Douglas Kellner and Jeff Share

Foreword by

Allan Luke

BRILL

SENSE

LEIDEN | BOSTON

Library of Congress Cataloging-in-Publication Data

Names: Kellner, Douglas, 1943- author. | Share, Jeff, author.
Title: The critical media literacy guide : engaging media and transforming
  education / by Douglas Kellner and Jeff Share.
Description: Leiden ; Boston : Brill Sense, [2019] | Series: Brill guides to
  scholarship in education, ISSN 2590-1958 ; volume 2 | Includes
  bibliographical references and index.
Identifiers: LCCN 2019014367 (print) | LCCN 2019016527 (ebook) | ISBN
  9789004404533 (ebook) | ISBN 9789004404519 (hardback : alk. paper) | ISBN
  9789004404526 (pbk. : alk. paper)
Subjects: LCSH: Media literacy--Study and teaching. | Mass media in
  education. | Critical pedagogy.
Classification: LCC P96.M4 (ebook) | LCC P96.M4 K45 2019 (print) | DDC
  302.23--dc23
LC record available at https://lccn.loc.gov/2019014367

Typeface for the Latin, Greek, and Cyrillic scripts: "Brill". See and download: brill.com/brill-typeface.

ISSN 2590-1958
ISBN 978-90-04-40452-6 (paperback)
ISBN 978-90-04-40451-9 (hardback)
ISBN 978-90-04-40453-3 (e-book)

Contents

Foreword

Allan Luke

Whether you are a school teacher or principal, teacher educator or researcher, or scholar interested in working with schools, children and young people – *The Critical Media Literacy Guide* explains practical tools for making sense of media, culture and politics, and everyday life. In an era of dizzying ideological indoctrination and propaganda, in a world of everyday battles for new digital and traditional media corporate survival, profit and hegemony, of increasing political and cultural conflict – all played out in a normative communicative context of disinformation, misrepresentation and outright lies – the case for a critical media literacy should go without saying. Yet calls for old and new normative ideals of truth and honesty, civility and ethical integrity, coherence and relevance in speech, print and digital communications often fall upon deaf ears, written off as Luddite anachronisms, empty clichés that hang suspended in a 24/7 environment where each claim and exchange is treated as ephemeral, transient and dated before the next tweet, message or video.

This is a moment where longstanding economic, geopolitical and intercultural settlements have come undone, where the digitalization of information, exchange and social relations have created an accelerated and micrometric media environment where no truth or untruth, claim or counterclaim goes unreported, unsurveilled, unresold and endlessly recycled – appearing and disappearing and appearing yet again in a digital archive that is at once everywhere and nowhere – while corporate and state power operate at scope and scale that we struggle to see, understand and comprehend. It is a world where the views of conspiracy theorists, internet influencers, weirdo pundits and bloggers sit alongside those of scientists, politicians, journalists, scholars, your next-door neighbors and everyone else. In this universe, meta-digital work undertaken by trolls, hackers, critics are lumped and melded together into a continuously renewed semiotic slurry that is opaque, unpredictable, and ubiquitous.

Meanwhile print schooling and curricula carry on in slumber, insulated from the ubiquitous texts and messages that have come to dominate everyday life. Kids are told to leave their phones elsewhere and carry on filling out worksheets; public policy debates focus on the latest phonics war and whether to arm teachers; print and digital edubusinesses vie for markets and clients, while teachers in economically stretched communities reach into their own pockets to supply their students with the basic requisites of print pedagogy: pencils, pens, stationary, books and, yes, crayons – while middle class parents reinvent parenting as continuous digital curation, surveillance and management of screen time, aspiring to the occasional meal, outing or conversation without device-in-hand.

In this world – to not teach an approach to critical literacy, a learned, informed and curious skepticism of a multimediated, multimodel information and textual environment – would be to walk away from any possibility of democratic education: the responsibility to teach each generation the tenets, values and stances that might enable us to live ethically, gainfully, and sustainably with diversity and difference and in shared purpose, fair and equitable exchange, and just community. This will require a rediscovery of quiet and sustained reflection, comparative and triangulated analyses of information, close and detailed reading and viewing, respect for difference, diversity and disagreement of ideas and ways of life, rich foundational and disciplinary knowledge, intergenerational wisdom and informed self-understanding – all easily written off as retrograde, old hat, too conservative, too radical, or, simply, too hard in a system that has put its time and money into standardised testing of basic skills.

Australian communications scholar and musician Phil Graham (in press/2019) recently commented:

> We undoubtedly know far more about how children learn to count than we do about how they learn to hate. We know far more about how a child acquires literacy than we do about how they acquire their sense of morality. That is more than likely a hangover from the scientific extremism of the early 20th century.

The approach to critical media literacy proposed by Douglas Kellner and Jeff Share addresses both these issues: This book is about teaching and learning how to decode, comprehend, critically engage with and produce the texts of everyday life, *and* it is about learning how to live ethically and sustainably in media culture, civil society and a planetary environment under threat. As they point out, the agenda for a critical media literacy is not new – and we need to quit treating it as some kind of radical innovation in traditional industrial/print schooling. For the debate confronting moral panic of new media arose first with the advent of radio and film in the early 20th century, then hit its stride with the emergence of TV in the postwar era (Luke, 1990) – while the systematic use of mass media for ideological propaganda, nationalism and military mobilisation, no stranger to print moguls from Pulitzer and Hearst to Murdoch, was first deployed by government in the WWI-era (Graham, 2017). So the use of mass media for purposes of large scale ideological mobilisation, the grafting of ideology and entertainment, and the use of the large scale media spectacle have and continue to play a key role in geopolitics and nationalism, the formation of identity and society, and, indeed, the rationalization of the strong state and authoritarianism.

What is different about this book are the unique foundational resources, perspectives and professional experience that are brought to the task by Douglas Kellner and Jeff Share. This is neither third party, dis-interested 'gold standard' science nor work by armchair academics. The authors are Los Angeles-based educators and activists who have committed decades of their lives and work to political and cultural struggle. They bring unique depth and experience to the task. Douglas Kellner is amongst the major social philosophers of this generation. He has never played it safe in the cloistered hallways of academic philosophy. Having established himself as one of the key American theorists working in the Frankfurt School tradition in the last century, he made a deliberate and unusual shift to the field of educational philosophy and to working with teachers in the past two decades. The result is a remarkable series of philosophic and political interventions – ranging from forensic work on American electoral fraud, to critiques of expanded militarism, important work on gun violence and masculinity in schooling, and trenchant analyses of the return of the authoritarian personality in American politics. Throughout this powerful corpus of critical work is a focus on media and its pedagogical role in the reshaping of American life and culture. For Douglas Kellner's Frankfurt school critique, critical media literacy is a positive thesis, a normative *praxis* for working with the next generation in ways that might regenerate and rebuild democratic society, ethical communications and social justice.

Jeff Share brings a remarkable life of work with and within media as a community activist and teacher with extensive experience across Mexico, Argentina and the Americas, and as an award-winning photojournalist, whose photographs have appeared in the *LA Times, Time, Rolling Stone, Mother Jones* and other major media outlets. His work has been recognized through the World Press Photo Oskar Barnack Award, Interpress Photo/World Peace Council Award, and the Olive Branch Award from the World Press Alliance for Nuclear Disarmament. He has prepared numerous photographic exhibitions for activist and international aid organisations. Jeff Share's work and life have focused on social justice, peace and intercultural exchange. But it was his bilingual/bicultural primary school teaching with LA minority communities and over a decade training new teachers that really brought this rich and diverse experience to ground. So he approaches the task from a unique perspective – as activist, as journalist, as photographer, as parent and as teacher working across and between cultures and languages. Jeff Share has pushed the boundaries of teaching and activism to their critical thresholds – and this book continues that journey.

As you sit back and tuck into this book, bear in mind the interesting life histories and expertise behind the analysis. For Kellner and Share, this is no simple academic or theoretical chess game – it is their answer to the urgent questions about what is to be done in educational systems and communities which find democratic institutions, cultural and linguistic traditions, work and social relations, and their very futures under a cloud of uncertainty. It is about how we might use communications media – from face-to-face talk to visual and graphic arts, from the writing of stories and essays to mastery of new digital modes of communication – to make and remake lives, communities and civil society in the face of unprecedented economic, cultural and political and indeed, ecological conditions. It's all on the line here.

Allan Luke
Brisbane, Australia
17 February 2019

Introduction

The convergence of information, media, and technology has created the predominant ecosystem of our time. Since 2018, more than half of the world's population (over 4 billion people) are using the Internet. From cradle to grave, we are interconnected through a globally-networked media and consumer society.

Media and information communication technologies can entertain, educate, and empower or distract, mislead, and manipulate. They are a profound and often misperceived source of cultural pedagogy that educate and socialize us about how to behave and what to think, feel, believe, fear, and desire. These complex systems of communication, representation, production, distribution, and consumption are forms of pedagogy that teach us about ourselves and the world around us. This is also an ecosystem that is constantly tracking and selling our movements, communications, and personal data. Therefore, learning how to question, analyze, and maneuver in this cultural environment are essential requirements for critical thinking and participatory democracy.

Radio, television, film, cell phones, popular music, the Internet, social networking, and other forms and products of media culture provide materials out of which we forge our sense of selfhood; our notions of gender; our conceptions of class, of ethnicity and race, of nationality, and of sexuality. Media culture shapes our views of the world into categories of "us" and "them," influencing our deepest values: what we consider good or bad, positive or negative, moral or evil. Media narratives provide the symbols, myths, and resources through which we constitute a common culture and through the appropriation of which we insert ourselves into this culture. Media spectacles demonstrate and legitimize who has power and who is powerless, who is allowed to exercise force and violence, and who suffers the consequences of it.

We have written this book to promote critical media literacy as a theoretical framework and practical pedagogy in order to enhance individual sovereignty vis-à-vis media culture, empowering people to critically read, write, and create a better world. Indeed, the realities of 21st century life, and the technological and information revolutions which characterize it, demand that all citizens become media literate. In fact, many universities are expanding and opening up their cinema/television courses to the university at large due to rising demands for these kinds of analytical and practical skills, which are hardly restricted any more to those looking for careers in the entertainment industry. In particular, the pedagogy of critical media literacy should be an essential part of all education. Unfortunately, this is not the case. Too many educational institutions ignore or undervalue the significance of critical media literacy as a crucial dimension of the knowledge, skills, and awareness necessary for 21st century literacy.

This book is designed for undergraduate and graduate students, K-12 teachers and university professors, as well as a general audience who is interested in critical media studies. It provides an introductory framework for understanding and decoding all forms of media culture from a critical perspective. Rather than separating different types of media into generic categories, this text introduces readers to critical theories and practices which are applicable to all forms of media and emphasizes the underlying similarities and unique qualities of each.

As technology continues to evolve, new potential emerges for positive and negative uses. Recent developments of machine learning, artificial intelligence, and augmented reality are creating the ability for more people to manipulate digital information, leading to impressive computer-generated imagery (CGI) in blockbuster movies, and also to the growth of fake news, doctored images, and misleading videos that go viral around the world in milliseconds.

While new information communication technologies (ICTs) have created potent opportunities for sharing and connecting people across the planet, they have also concentrated access and control of information, and have produced digital divides and information inequalities. Today's primary storytellers are enormous transnational corporations merging and expanding globally to almost every corner of the planet, and locally to every nook and cranny they can reach. Only a handful of corporations own the majority of the world's media, creating a small group of wealthy oligarchs and plutocrats with tremendous power to decide who and what will be represented and what lessons will be taught by the largest cultural industry the world has ever known (McChesney & Nichols, 2016).

When a small number of corporations have the power to create and disseminate enormous amounts of information, the diversity of ideas shrinks as the potential for abuse increases. Media consolidation is especially problematic when the majority of the audience perceives the messages and media through which they travel as neutral and transparent. Taking media culture for granted promotes a relationship with media in which messages are rarely questioned or challenged, especially when they are considered entertainment.

At the same time, social media are providing new possibilities for individuals and groups to find each other and build grassroots coalitions. The Arab Spring, Black Lives Matter, and the #MeToo movement are powerful examples of the potential social media offer for connecting, organizing, and challenging systems of oppression. Yet, the social networking that brings like-minded people together is also being used to foment anger, hatred, and physical violence. These days, all types of groups, from the Islamic State to American street gangs, are using social media to find followers and spread their own agendas and beliefs, thereby turning social media into weapons of warfare (Singer & Brooking, 2018).

Awareness and engagement through critical inquiry, therefore, becomes an essential requirement for literacy and education in the 21st century. As a response to changes in technology, media, and society, education and citizenship today require the development of critical media literacy (CML) to empower students and citizens to critically read media messages and produce media themselves in order to be active participants in a democratic society. This necessitates awareness of how media function in everyday life and developing critical literacies to decode crucial meanings, messages, and effects. Much of the daily public pedagogy that mass media (which includes social media) teach about race, gender, class, sexuality, consumption, fear, morals, and the like, reflect corporate profit motives and hegemonic ideologies at the expense of social concerns necessary for a healthy democracy and a sustainable planet.

Since traditional education often does little to help students recognize and counteract these influences, we need a more robust type of literacy that *expands* critical consciousness to encompass new ICTs, media, and popular culture and *deepens* pedagogical practices to more complex levels in order to question the relationships between information and power. Critical awareness is akin to what Paulo Freire (2010) calls *conscientização*, a revolutionary critical consciousness that involves perception as well as action against oppression. Critical awareness in CML involves identifying, analyzing, and challenging media that promote representations or narratives involving racism, sexism, classism, homophobia and other forms of discrimination that further marginalize targeted social groups.

Through this expansion of literacy and deepening of critical inquiry, CML aims to challenge popular assumptions that frame media as unproblematic windows to the world. An essential concept of media literacy is the social construction of knowledge and the ramifications of that understanding to disrupt misconceptions of information and education as neutral and bias-free. This critical pedagogical approach to literacy offers the dual possibility of building awareness of media domination through critical analysis and empowering individuals to create alternative media for counter-hegemonic expression. CML pedagogy provides students and teachers with an opportunity to embrace the changes in society and technology, not as threats to education, but as opportunities to rethink teaching and learning as political acts of consciousness-raising and empowerment.

Hence, as traditional educational systems promote oppressive practices that focus more on conformity and memorization than critical thinking and empowerment, we need a progressive educational response to challenge these harmful influences and provide a positive alternative to humanize and democratize education. The current obsession with standardization and accountability are prioritizing misleading notions of success and equality at the expense of students' and society's social and environmental needs. Democracy, social justice, and the fate of life on this planet require education that prepares everyone to work in solidarity to create a more humane, sustainable, and compassionate world. Teachers should guide students to challenge status quo practices and dominant ideologies that support racism, sexism, classism, homophobia, overconsumption, and all forms of oppression and exploitation.

While pressures to privatize and standardize education have been building, a dramatic technological revolution, centered on computers, information, communication, and multimedia technologies, has been changing everything from the ways people work, to the ways they communicate with each other and spend their leisure time. This ICT eruption is often interpreted as the beginnings of a knowledge or information society, and therefore ascribes education a central role in every aspect of life. It poses tremendous challenges to educators to rethink their basic tenets, to deploy the new technologies in creative and productive ways, and to restructure schooling to respond constructively and progressively to the technological and social changes that we are now experiencing. At the same time that this ICT shift is underway, important demographic, socio-political, and environmental changes are taking place in the United States and throughout the world. Immigration patterns have created the challenge of providing people from diverse cultures, classes, and backgrounds with the tools and competencies to enable them to succeed and participate in an ever more complex and multicultural world. Additionally, as the climate continues to warm, more people will be forced to leave their countries in search of the basic human needs no longer sustainable in their homelands.

Digital technology is opening opportunities for individual participation and alternative points of view, while at the same time, a few enormous media and technology corporations have become the dominant chroniclers, narrators, and gatekeepers of information, often repeating the same story, at the expense of countless different perspectives and creative ways of thinking. Many of these storytellers are actually story-sellers, more interested in peddling ideas and products, than informing, enlightening, inspiring, or encouraging critical thinking. While children are using more media, they are also being used more by media companies. These giant transnational media and technology corporations are capturing personal data and targeting youth as one of the most valuable markets to build brand loyalty and to sell to advertisers or anyone willing to pay.

Researchers found that 8–18 year-olds in the US spend well over ten hours a day interacting with various forms of media, such as music, computers, video games, television, film, and print (Rideout, Lauricella, & Wartella, 2011). Another investigation reports "45% of teens say they are online on a near-constant basis" and "[a]nother 44% say they go online several times a day, meaning roughly nine-in-ten teens go online at least multiple times per day" (Anderson & Jiang, 2018, p. 8). Much of this media use is attributed to easy access, since 95% of US teens surveyed report having their own smartphone or access to one (p. 2). This increase in access and use of cell phones, tablets, and digital media is leading some researchers to assert that the constantly increasing amount of information, the lightning speed and immediacy with which it arrives, the high levels of stimulation and multitasking that consume us as we read, are distracting us from being able to focus our attention enough to read deeply and think critically (Carr, 2014; Turkle, 2011, 2015; Wolf, 2018). Maryanne Wolf (2018) further suggests that digital culture has created a threat to empathy, diversity, and democracy through "continuous partial attention" that is rewiring our brain's circuitry (p. 71).

Not only is the amount of time with media increasing, but the quality of that engagement is also changing, becoming more commercial and rarely critical. In 2016, researchers at Stanford University assessed 7,804 students across the US on their competence to analyze online media and report that, "young people's ability to reason about the information on the Internet can be summed up in one word: bleak" (p. 4). The researchers found that students are "easily duped" and unprepared to distinguish between news and advertising or to judge the reliability of a website. They assert, "Never have we had so much information at our fingertips. Whether this bounty will make us smarter and better informed or more ignorant and narrow-minded will depend on our awareness of this problem and our educational response to it" (Stanford History Education Group, 2016, p. 5). The vast amount of information we encounter every day, the ubiquity of social media and online connectivity, our dependence on cell phones and digital technology, the commercial structure of the information highway, and the convergence of information, communication, and entertainment are creating the need for pedagogy that will support students to critically negotiate this dynamic terrain. The new digital culture presents potential dangers when ICTs are used without analysis and reflection, and they also offer positive possibilities when they are used critically for educating, empowering, and engaging in social and environmental justice.

In our constantly evolving society, media and technology continue to assert evermore influence in shaping culture, disseminating ideas, and determining public discourse. The synergy between entertainment and politics is profound and can be seen in examples such as Barack Obama's 2008 presidential campaign winning the top prizes at the Cannes Lions International Advertising Awards. When political campaigns win advertising awards, democracy has taken a backseat to the media spectacle (Kellner, 2003). These changes are contributing to the need for everyone to develop the skills and disposition to question and respond to the information they are hearing, seeing, reading, creating, sharing, and using.

Another issue for educators to embrace is the rise of fake news (purposefully fictitious media posts) and the cooptation of the term "fake news" by Trump and conservatives. Hence, a label that was once useful to identify false information, has now become a tool of propaganda and disinformation. Early in his presidency, Donald Trump declared a "war on the media" in his daily twitter feed and media appearances, using the concept of "fake news" to discredit media reports critical of him (Kellner, 2017). Trump and his staff dismiss reporting they don't approve of as "fake news" and attack the mainstream press, referring to them as "the true Enemy of the People" (Trump's tweet, October 29, 2018). Along with his attacks on mainstream news media, Trump's level of "purposefully injecting false information into the national discourse" has prompted the Washington Post Fact Checker to introduce a new category called the Bottomless Pinocchio, which overtakes the previously lowest rating of four Pinocchios, given for a claim that is proven false. Glenn Kessler (2018) explains that the Bottomless Pinocchio, "will be awarded to politicians who repeat a false claim so many times that they are, in effect, engaging in campaigns of disinformation."

The use of the term "fake news" for political gain, along with the increase in false information spread through social media by online bots, click farms, troll factories, and sockpuppets has encouraged many people to recognize the need to develop critical reading skills of media and contemporary discourses, debates, and controversies. However, some have suggested that we simply need better cognitive skills and critical awareness to determine truth from lies. If only it were that simple. The development of new technology is also contributing to the potential to manipulate facts, remix media, and create "deep fake" videos that look convincingly real (Chesney & Citron, 2018). Making sense of media and our information society is far more complicated than a reductionist idea of simply finding the truth. Rather than judging information in binary terms, as either true or false, students should learn to seek context, search for multiple sources, different perspectives, and various types of evidence, to triangulate findings and bias in order to best evaluate and make sense of the information.

Yet, in this toxic political environment, we must avoid relativistic suggestions that everything is equal and we are in a post-truth era because real events occur that affect people and all life on the planet. Joe Kincheloe (2007) reminds us that "all knowledge is an interpretation" (p. 113) and therefore, interpreting the meaning of a message is a complex process that requires skills to probe empirical evidence, evaluate subjective biases, analyze the medium and construction of the text, and explore the multiple meanings and social contexts of media texts. Simply labeling a text as "real" or "fake" is overly simplistic and does little to help understand our media culture and become an adept and critical user and/or producer of information in the public discourse.

Journalists Bill Kovach and Tom Rosenstiel (2011) assert that changes in technology and journalism have shifted our relationship with news, from a "trust me" era of the mainstream media being given the authority to tell us what we need to know, to the current "show me" era that places the onus of judging the news more on us as the audience. Kovach and Rosenstiel (2011) write, "That reflects the power shift in the digital age from the journalist as gatekeeper to the consumer or citizen as his or her own editor. With that shift the consumer has now acquired a greater responsibility to adopt and perfect a skeptical way of knowing" (p. 33). While we can question if it was a good idea to have given so much power to journalists in the first place, perhaps the new challenges of the digital age will provoke us to become more responsible and skeptical citizens and users, discussants, and producers of news and information.

Now, more than ever, teachers should encourage students to be reading, viewing, listening to, interacting with, and creating a multitude of texts, from books and articles, to digital podcasts and multimedia productions. This is an opportunity for educators to guide their students to think critically with and about the information technology and media that surround them. Hence, changes in media, technology, and society require critical media literacy that can support teachers and students to question and create *with* and *about* all forms of communication that can empower or oppress, entertain or distract, inform or mislead, and buy or sell everything from lifestyles to politicians.

Critical media literacy is a pedagogical approach that deepens literacy skills across all subject areas and empowers students to use multiple forms of media and technology to read and write the word and the world (Freire & Macedo, 1987). In this brave new world of exploding media and computer technologies, we need to rethink education, literacy, and our roles as educators. While media literacy courses have been taught and appreciated in select parts of the world, in the US, advocates of critical media literacy have been a marginalized, yet growing group. It is obvious to us that new ICTs require new literacies and that schools today must confront the challenges of providing appropriate forms of education and teach the literacies that enable students and citizens to thrive in the 21st century.

In this book, we argue that educators need to cultivate critical media literacy to meet the challenge of restructuring education for a digitally-networked multicultural society and global culture. In a period of dramatic technological, social, and environmental change, education needs to help produce a variety of new types of literacies to make current pedagogy relevant to the demands of the contemporary era. As new ICTs are altering every aspect of our society and culture, we need to comprehend and make use of them to understand and transform our world. In particular, by introducing critical media literacy to empower individuals and groups traditionally excluded, education can be reconstructed to make it more responsive to the challenges of a democratic and multicultural society.

Towards Critical Digital and Media Literacies

To dramatize the issues at stake, we should consider the claim that we are now undergoing one of the most significant technological revolutions since the progression from oral to print and book-based teaching (Best & Kellner, 2001; Castells, 1996). Just as the transition to print literacy and book culture involved a dramatic transformation of education (McLuhan, 1962, 2003; Ong, 1995), so too does the ongoing technological revolution demand a major restructuring of education today with new curricula, pedagogy, literacies, practices, and goals. Furthermore, the technological revolution of the present era makes possible the radical reconstruction of education and society argued for in the progressive era by John Dewey and in the post-1960s era by Ivan Illich, Paulo Freire, bell hooks, and others who sought radical educational and social reform.

Put in historical perspective, it is now possible to see modern education as preparation for industrial civilization and minimal citizenship in a passive representative democracy with citizens as spectators of media spectacles. However, the demands of the expanding global economy, culture, and polity require a more informed, participatory, and active workforce and citizenship, and thus increased roles and challenges for education. Modern education, in short, emphasizes submission to authority, rote memorization, and what Freire (2010) calls the "banking concept" of education, in which teachers deposit knowledge into passive students, inculcating conformity, subordination, normalization, and regurgitation. These traits are becoming obsolete in a global postindustrial and networked society with its demands for new skills for the workplace, participation in emergent social and political environs, and interaction within novel forms of culture and everyday life.

A more flexible economy, based on an ever-evolving technological infrastructure and more multicultural workforce demands a more technically and critically literate, interactive, culturally sensitive, and educated workforce; while revitalizing democracy requires the participation of informed citizens. Thus, constant technological revolution renders necessary the sort of thorough restructuring of education that radicals demanded during the last century, indeed back to the Enlightenment if one includes Rousseau and Wollstonecraft, who saw the progressive restructuring of education as the key to democracy. Today, however, intense pressures for change come more often from technology and the economy and less frequently from education reform. With an expanding global economy and novel technologies demanding innovative skills, competencies, literacies, and practices, today's economy requires new literacies. While this technological revolution has highly ambiguous effects, it provides educational reformers with the challenge of whether education will be restructured to promote democracy and human needs, or whether education will be transformed primarily to serve the interests of business and the global economy.

It is therefore a burning question, what sort of restructuring will take place, in whose interests, and for what ends. More than ever, we need philosophical reflection on the ends and purposes of education, on what we are doing and trying to achieve in our educational practices and institutions. In this situation, it may be instructive to return to John Dewey and see the connections between education and democracy, the need for the reconstruction of education and society, and the value of experimental pedagogy to seek solutions to the problems of education in the present day (1916/1997 and 1938/1963). A progressive reconstruction of education will urge that it be done in the interests of democratization, ensuring access to new technologies for all, and training in the digital and media literacies necessary to master the new technologies. This restructuring of education will help students and citizens to overcome the so-called digital divide and divisions of the haves and have nots, so that education is placed, as Dewey (1916/1997) and Freire (2010) propose, in the service of democracy and social justice.

Yet we should be more aware than Dewey of the persistence of divisions of class, gender, and race, and work self-consciously for multicultural democracy and education. This task suggests that we valorize difference and cultural specificity, as well as shared universal Deweyean values such as freedom, equality, individualism, and participation. Theorizing a democratic and multicultural reconstruction of education forces us to confront the digital divide, that there are divisions between information and technology have and have nots, just as there are class, gender, and race divisions in every sphere of the existing constellations of society and culture.

With the proper resources, policies, pedagogies, and practices, educators can work to reduce the (unfortunately growing) gap between haves and have nots by promoting broad training in critical media literacy. This training must not only provide access but the ability to use and reconstruct new technologies and media to engage in social discussion, media production and creation, and socio-political participation in contemporary society. The students in the Parkland, Florida shooting, for instance, have used their media skills to protest lax gun laws and to mobilize students and others to participate in political demonstrations and campaigns to change gun laws and elect a more responsive Congress (Hogg & Hogg, 2018).

Hence, critical media and digital literacies embrace a wide range of projects, from providing technical skills to engaging students in the analysis, production, and use of media. Although technology alone will not suffice to democratize and adequately reconstruct education in a technological society, providing proper access and training can improve education if it is taken as a supplement. That is, technology itself does not necessarily improve teaching and learning, and will certainly not of itself overcome acute socio-economic divisions. Indeed, without proper resources, pedagogy, and educational practices, technology could be an obstacle or burden to genuine learning and will probably increase rather than overcome existing divisions of power, cultural capital, and wealth.

In the following chapters, we focus on the role of critical media literacy (CML) to expand the concept of literacy and reconstruct education in order to prepare students to respond to the increase in media and ICTs in every aspect of life. We also propose some ways in which new ICTs and CML can serve as powerful forms of education that can contribute to producing a more democratic and egalitarian society, not just providing skills and tools to privileged individuals and groups that will improve their cultural capital and social power at the expense of others.

Media Literacy: An Unfulfilled Challenge

Literacy involves gaining the skills and knowledge to read and interpret the texts of the world and to successfully navigate and negotiate its challenges, conflicts, and crises. Literacy is thus a necessary condition to equip people to participate in the local, national, and global economy, culture, and polity. As Dewey argues (1997), education is necessary to enable people to participate in democracy, for without an educated, informed, and literate citizenry, strong democracy is impossible. Moreover, there are crucial links between literacy, democracy, empowerment, and participation, and without developing adequate literacies, differences between haves and have nots cannot be overcome, and individuals and groups will be left out of the emerging economy, networked society, and global culture, thereby subject to ever-worse conditions of poverty, social and environmental degradation, and multiple forms of oppression.

In addition to reading, writing, and traditional print literacies, one could argue that in an era of technological revolution, we need to develop robust forms of critical media literacy, computer literacy, and multimedia literacies, thus cultivating "multiple literacies" in the restructuring of education. Computer and multimedia technologies demand novel skills and competencies, and if education is to be relevant to the problems and challenges of contemporary life, it must expand the concept of literacy and develop new curricula and pedagogies.

Traditionalists and reformists would probably agree that education and literacy are intimately connected. "Literacy" in our conception comprises gaining competencies and awareness involved in effectively using socially-constructed forms of communication and representation. Learning literacies involves attaining competencies in contexts that are governed by rules and conventions. Literacies are socially constructed in educational and cultural practices involved in various institutional discourses and practices. Literacies evolve and shift in response to social and cultural change and the interests of elites who control hegemonic institutions.

We should resist, however, extreme claims that the era of the book and print literacy are over. Although there are discontinuities and novelties in the current constellation, there are also important continuities. Indeed, in the emergent ICT environment, traditional print literacy takes on increasing importance in the computer-mediated cyberworld, as people need to critically scrutinize and scroll tremendous amounts of information, putting new emphasis on developing reading and writing abilities. For instance, Internet discussion groups, chat rooms, e-mail, blogs, tweets, and all forms of social media require reading and writing skills in which a new emphasis on the importance of clarity and precision is emerging. In this context of information saturation, it becomes an ethical imperative not to contribute to cultural and information overload, and to concisely communicate thoughts and feelings.

In the new multimedia environment, critical media literacy is arguably more important than ever. Cultural studies and critical pedagogy have begun to teach us to recognize the ubiquity of media culture in contemporary society, and the growing need for culturally sustaining pedagogies (Paris & Alim, 2017) in an environment in which immigrants, people of color, and the poor are under attack by rightwing governments throughout the world. In this global context, the need for media literacy that addresses the issue of multicultural and social difference and that aims at social and environmental justice becomes all the more important. There is expanding recognition that media representations help construct our images and understanding of the world and that education must meet the dual challenges of teaching media literacy in a multicultural society and sensitizing students and publics to the inequities and injustices of a society based on gender, race, and class inequalities and discrimination. Recent critical studies see the role of mainstream media in exacerbating or diminishing these inequalities and the ways that critical media education and the production of alternative media can help create a healthy multiculturalism of diversity and a more robust democracy. They confront some of the most serious difficulties and problems that currently face us as educators and citizens.

Yet, despite the ubiquity of media culture in contemporary society and everyday life, and the recognition that media themselves are a form of pedagogy, and despite criticisms of the distorted values, ideals, and representations of the world in popular culture, media education in K-12 schooling has never been systematically established and developed in the United States. The current technological revolution, however, brings to the fore more than ever the role of media such as television, cell phones, popular music, film, video games, digital platforms, and advertising, as the Internet rapidly absorbs these cultural forms and creates new cyberspaces and forms of culture and pedagogy. It is highly irresponsible, in the face of saturation by Internet and media culture, to ignore these forms of socialization and education; consequently, a critical reconstruction of education should produce pedagogies that provide critical media literacy and enable students, teachers, and citizens to discern the nature and effects of media culture.

Media culture is a type of pedagogy that teaches proper and improper behavior, gender roles, values, and knowledge of the world. Individuals are often not aware that they are being educated and constructed by media culture, as its pedagogy is frequently invisible and subliminal. This situation calls for critical approaches that make us aware of how media construct meanings, influence and educate audiences, and impose their messages and values. A media literate person is skillful in analyzing media codes and conventions, able to criticize stereotypes, values, and ideologies, and competent to interpret and create multiple meanings and messages. Media literacy helps people to use media intelligently, to discriminate and evaluate media content, to critically dissect media forms, to investigate media effects and uses, and to produce media messages in various formats.

Within educational circles, however, a debate persists over what constitutes the field of media pedagogy, with different agendas and programs. A traditionalist "protectionist" approach would attempt to "inoculate" young people against the effects of media addiction and manipulation by cultivating a taste for book literacy, high culture, and the values of truth, beauty, and justice, and by denigrating all forms of media and computer culture (Postman, 1985). A "media literacy" movement, by contrast, attempts to teach students to read, analyze, and decode media texts, in the fashion of the typical psychological model of print literacy (Luke & Freebody, 1997). Media arts education, in turn, teaches students to appreciate the aesthetic qualities of media and to use various media technologies as instruments of self-expression and creation.

Critical media literacy builds on these approaches, analyzing media culture as products of social production and struggle, and teaching students to be critical of media representations and ideologies, while also stressing the importance of learning to use the media as modes of self-expression and social activism (Kellner, 1995; Share, 2015a).

Developing critical media literacy pedagogy also involves perceiving how any type of media can be used positively to teach a wide range of topics, such as multicultural understandings of ethnic and racial diversity, problems of discrimination and oppression around the axis of race, gender, sexuality, and religion, and the need for education to be devoted to social and environmental justice. If, for example, education is to champion genuine diversity and expand the curriculum, it is important for groups excluded from mainstream education to learn about their own heritage and for dominant groups to explore the experiences and voices of minority and marginalized groups. Thus, critical media literacy can promote multicultural literacy, conceived as understanding and engaging the heterogeneity of cultures and subcultures that constitute an increasingly global and multicultural world, as well as promoting understanding of the differences, challenges and forms of oppression organized around class, race, gender, and sexuality.

Critical media literacy not only teaches students to learn from media, to resist media manipulation, and to use media materials in constructive ways, but is also concerned with developing skills that will help create responsible citizens who are motivated and competent participants in social-political life. Critical media literacy is tied to the project of radical participatory democracy and is concerned about developing skills that will enhance democratization and participation. It takes a comprehensive approach that teaches critical skills and how to use media as instruments of social communication and change. The technologies of communication are becoming more and more accessible to young people and ordinary citizens, and can be used to promote education, democratic self-expression, and social progress. Technologies that could help produce the end of participatory democracy, by transforming politics into media spectacles and a battle of images, and by turning spectators into cultural zombies, could also be used to help invigorate democratic debate and participation.

Indeed, teaching critical media literacy could be a participatory, collaborative project. Watching films or online postings together could promote productive discussions between teachers and students (or parents and children), with emphasis on eliciting student views, producing a variety of interpretations of media texts and teaching basic principles of hermeneutics and criticism. Students and youth are often more media savvy, knowledgeable, and immersed in media culture than their teachers, and can contribute to the educational process through sharing their ideas, perceptions, and insights. Critical discussion, debate, and analysis ought to be encouraged, with teachers posing salient questions and bringing to bear critical perspectives on student readings of media material. Since media culture is often part and parcel of students' identity and most powerful cultural experiences, teachers must be sensitive in criticizing artifacts and perceptions that students hold dear because an atmosphere of critical respect for difference *and* inquiry into the nature and effects of media culture should be promoted.

A major challenge in developing critical media literacy, however, results from the fact that it is not a pedagogy in the traditional sense, with firmly-established principles, a canon of texts, and tried-and-true teaching procedures. Critical media pedagogy is in its infancy; it is just beginning to develop, and is more open and experimental than established print-oriented pedagogy. Moreover, the technologies and material of media culture are so multivalent and polysemic, subject to multiple interpretations, that they necessitate sensitivity to different readings, interpretations, and perceptions of the complex images, scenes, narratives, meanings, and messages of media culture, which in its own way is as complex and challenging to critically decipher as book culture. Further, we need to appreciate that individuals perceive and experience sexism, racism, classism, homophobia, and other forms of biases in media differently, according to their own class, gender, racial, sexual, and subject positions.

Teaching critical media literacy involves occupation of a site above the dichotomy of fandom or censor. One can teach how media culture spreads significant statements or insights about the social world, empowering visions of gender, race, and class, or complex aesthetic structures and practices, thereby putting a positive spin on how it can provide significant contributions to education. Yet we ought to indicate also how media culture can advance sexism, racism, ethnocentrism, classism, homophobia, and other forms of prejudice, as well as misinformation, problematic ideologies, and questionable values. By exploring positive and negative influences of media culture, we promote a dialectical and critical approach that views media as forms of information and misinformation, potential knowledge and miseducation. In the following chapters we advance a concept of critical media literacy that engages problems of gender, race, class, sexuality, and other key elements of identities and forms of oppression and discrimination in contemporary media and technological societies.

Overview of Critical Media Literacy

Evolving from the multidisciplinary field of cultural studies and critical educational pedagogies, critical media literacy aims to *expand* our understanding of literacy to include reading and writing of all types of texts, as well as to *deepen* analysis to more critical levels that examine the relationships between media and audiences, information and power. Critical media literacy constitutes a specific body of knowledge and set of skills, as well as a framework of *conceptual understandings* (Buckingham, 2003). Based on the work of many scholars and organizations around the world, the following is a list of six critical media literacy conceptual understandings and corresponding questions (Funk, Kellner, & Share, 2016).

These conceptual understandings and questions are intended to guide educators and students down a critical path of inquiry to interrogate any text, medium, and the context that surround it. As Kovach and Rosenstiel (2011)

Conceptual Understandings	Questions
1. *Social Constructivism* All information is co-constructed by individuals and/or groups of people who make choices within social contexts.	*WHO* are all the possible people who made choices that helped create this text?
2. *Languages/Semiotics* Each medium has its own language with specific grammar and semantics.	*HOW* was this text constructed and delivered/accessed?
3. *Audience/Positionality* Individuals and groups understand media messages similarly and/or differently depending on multiple contextual factors.	*HOW* could this text be understood differently?
4. *Politics of Representation* Media messages and the medium through which they travel always have a bias and support and/or challenge dominant hierarchies of power, privilege, and pleasure.	*WHAT* values, points of view, and ideologies are represented or missing from this text or influenced by the medium?
5. *Production/Institutions* All media texts have a purpose (often commercial or governmental) that is shaped by the creators and/or systems within which they operate.	*WHY* was this text created and/or shared?
6. *Social and Environmental Justice* Media culture is a terrain of struggle that perpetuates or challenges positive and/or negative ideas about people, groups, and issues; it is never neutral.	*WHOM* does this text advantage and/or disadvantage?

assert, "Asking questions begins the process of deconstructing the media content we see in front of us. Critical thinking is not a formula – it is a journey" (p. 210).

Much of the theory upon which critical media literacy is based has evolved from critical communications theories and cultural studies, fields of critical inquiry that began in the 20th century in Europe and continue to grow with new critiques of media and society. From the 1930s through the 1960s, researchers at the Frankfurt Institute for Social Research used critical social theory to analyze how media culture and the new tools of communication technology reproduce dominant forms of ideology and social control. In the 1960s, researchers at the Centre for Contemporary Cultural Studies at the University of Birmingham added to the earlier concerns of ideology with a more sophisticated understanding of the audience as active constructors of reality, not simply mirrors of an external reality, and expanded the concept of ideology to include race, gender, sexuality, and other components as well as class. Cultural studies has continued to grow and incorporate concepts of semiotics, feminism, multiculturalism, and postmodernism (Kellner, 1995). Incorporating a dialectical understanding of political economy, textual analysis, and audience theory, cultural studies critiques media culture as dynamic discourses that reproduce dominant ideologies as well as entertain, educate, and offer the possibilities for counterhegemonic alternatives.

The conceptual understandings of critical media literacy are most relevant to progressive education when taught through a democratic approach within critical pedagogy that follows ideas of transformative educators like Dewey and Freire. Without a critical framework encompassing a vision of education as a force to produce expanded participatory democracy, the core concepts can become tools for instrumental progressivism (Robins & Webster, 2001) and lose their transformative potential (Ferguson, 2004). As media education continues to evolve, it is essential that critical pedagogy be a central component and that CML be connected with social and environmental justice, participatory democracy, and progressive social transformation.

Pedagogical Antecedents of Critical Media Literacy

Dewey

John Dewey (1859–1952) stands out as a significant philosopher of education who contributed greatly to current understandings about progressive education. Antonia Darder, Marta Baltodano, and Rodolfo Torres (2003) write about the history of critical pedagogy and pay homage to Dewey as having "had a significant influence on progressive educators concerned with advancing democratic ideals in education" (p. 3). Dewey appreciated the power of the environment and considered understanding and connecting with the environment essential to education. He explains, "the environment consists of those conditions that promote or hinder, stimulate or inhibit, the *characteristic* activities of a living being" (Dewey, 1916/1997, p. 11). It is through acting upon the environment that Dewey asserts life becomes "a self-renewing process" (p. 2). For most students in the US today, a major part of their environment is media, and critical media literacy provides a direct path to act upon and transform that environment.

Dewey's progressive goals of democracy become practical through his pragmatic approach to teaching based upon experience. He insists, "Every experience is a moving force. Its value can be judged only on the ground of what it moves toward and into" (1938/1963, p. 38). Dewey envisions progressive education as a continual spiral where the teacher creates curiosity through structuring experiences for students to engage, explore, and experiment. As they actively challenge new experiences, their inquiry continues to spiral out into more questions and connections with more experiences. He explains:

> Unless a given experience leads out into a field previously unfamiliar no problems arise, while problems are the stimulus to thinking. That the conditions found in present experience should be used as sources of problems is a characteristic which differentiates education based upon experience from traditional education. (p. 79)

Dewey makes a distinction between experiential progressive education and traditional education that is concerned with social conformity and transmission of facts. In line with his goals of democracy, Dewey places great emphasis on the need for active learning, experimentation, and problem solving. He asserts that education will be interesting to students when they perceive a meaningful connection between themselves and the material. Dewey's pragmatic approach connects theory with practice and requires students to similarly connect reflection with action. In Dewey's words: "Numbers are not objects of study just because they are numbers already constituting a branch of learning called mathematics, but because they represent qualities and relations of the world in which our action goes on, because they are factors upon which the accomplishments of our purposes depends" (1916/1997, p. 134). For media education to be transformative, it must be taught through a critical pedagogy that recognizes:

> Knowledge is humanistic in quality not because it is about human prod-
> ucts in the past, but because of what it does in liberating human intelli-
> gence and human sympathy. Any subject matter which accomplishes this
> result is humane, and any subject matter which does not accomplish it is
> not even educational. (Dewey, 1916/1997, p. 230)

Transformative education requires a critical pedagogy of solidarity in which
empathy and compassion help students understand the ways people are interconnected through systems of dominance and subordination. Through combining media production with critical analysis, critical media literacy holds the
potential to create liberatory pedagogy.

Freire

Brazilian educator Paulo Freire (1921–1997) is another key figure in the development of progressive education and critical pedagogy. Darder and colleagues (2003) state, "Freire is considered by many to be the most influential
educational philosopher in the development of critical pedagogical thought
and practice" (p. 5). Both, Dewey and Freire were critical of the established
educational systems, proponents of progressive social change, and believers
in the need to unite theory with practice. However, Dewey's liberal reform
is less radical than Freire's revolutionary pedagogy based on liberation from
oppression. The two men saw humans as being in the process of evolving, and
education as an important tool to assist people in becoming more humane
and complete. While Dewey opposed dualism, Freire's dialectical perspective
defined freedom as the opposite of oppression. Freire (2010) asserts, "Concern
for humanization leads at once to the recognition of dehumanization, not only
as an ontological possibility but as an historical reality" (p. 43).

Freire's critical pedagogy is radically political in its call for *conscientização*, a
revolutionary critical consciousness that involves perception as well as action
against oppression. He proposes *problem-posing pedagogy* as a liberating alternative to the dehumanizing *banking education* that can still be found today
in most schools around the world. Freire describes banking education as an
alienating system that deposits fragments of information into passive students
like money into a bank. He explains that the real teaching accomplished by
banking education is a hidden curriculum that indoctrinates and pacifies, "for
the more the oppressed can be led to adapt to that situation, the more easily
they can be dominated" (p. 74).

The problem-posing alternative that Freire supports requires dialogical
communication between students and teachers, where both are learning and
teaching each other. He states (2010), "One must seek to live *with* others in

solidarity. One cannot impose oneself, nor even merely co-exist with one's students. Solidarity requires true communication" (pp. 76–77). This is a revolutionary act that necessitates *praxis*, critical reflection together with action to transform society. Freire writes, "In dialectical thought, world and action are intimately interdependent" (p. 53). The concept of praxis is an important reason that critical media literacy teaches students how to create media and critically participate in media culture as well as analyze media messages. Henry Jenkins (2006) asserts, "We need to rethink the goals of media education so that young people can come to think of themselves as cultural producers and participants and not simply as consumers, critical or otherwise" (p. 259).

Freire thus argues that students are shaped by schooling systems as passive recipients of knowledge rather than as producers and creators. Freire's work is renowned for his critique of the "banking" concept of education, in which student are viewed as empty recipients to be filled by the teacher. The banking concept of education "transforms students into receiving objects. It attempts to control thinking and action, leads men and women to adjust to the world, and inhibits their creative power" (p. 77). Further, Freire's description of "antidialogical mythicizing" explains how in order for the dominant minority to oppress the majority, they need to increase the alienation and passivity of the oppressed. This is achieved through hegemonic myths that are taught in schools, repeated in the media, and naturalized through the dominant society's worldview, such as the need to conform to authority to achieve success, or capitalist myths about the "free market" and competition as the best form of social organization to ensure prosperity for all.

Freire explains that the oppressive myths "are presented to them by well-organized propaganda and slogans, via the mass 'communications' media – as if such alienation constituted real communication" (p. 140). This understanding of the role media play in maintaining hegemony and oppression led Freire to suggest that problem-posing education needs to present these myths to students as problems to be unveiled through dialogue. He asserts (2010), "It is not the media themselves which I criticize, but the way they are used" (p. 140). Hence, critical media literacy can help students deconstruct the myths and take action to create counterhegemonic media whereby students become subjects, as opposed to objects, and name their world. Through denaturalizing media representations, students can expose the workings of ideology. However, it is not enough to just identify sexist, racist, classist, or homophobic messages or their origins; students should be encouraged to question how these oppressive ideologies are sustained and normalized, then create alternative readings that expose and challenge the ideological discourses and narratives.

Reconstructing Critical Media Literacy in the 21st Century

Previous critical pedagogies and development of media literacies took place in a 20th century social-economic world marked by industrial and techno-logical revolutions, growing differences between the haves and the have nots, periodic economic and social crises, and environmental degradation. Critical educators attempted to respond to these problems by empowering students to become citizens in a complex, evolving, world of challenges. As conflicts in different parts of the world intensified during the Cold War and in anti- and post-colonial movements throughout the Global South, internally, conflicts around race, class, gender, sexuality, religion, and political ideologies intensi-fied in developed democratic capitalist countries like the United States.

As we move into the third decade of the 21st century, we need to rethink and reconstruct education to make it relevant to the socio-cultural, economic, political, global, and environmental challenges of the contemporary era. One constant between the 20th and 21st centuries is intense technological devel-opment and ongoing social, political, and cultural challenges. Educators need to critically engage new technologies and social media to expand literacies from book to media to new digital literacies, teaching students and citizens to become empowered participants in the social struggles and crises of the contemporary moment.

Critical media and digital literacies need to engage conflicts around class and inequality, gender, racial and sexual oppression, religious discrimination, and political bias to teach students to become critical and discriminating readers of a variety of texts, from books, to broadcast media, to new digital media and social networking. Hence, literacies must be constantly evolving to embrace new technologies and forms of culture and communication, and must be critical, teaching students to become discerning readers, interpreters, and producers of media texts and new types of social communication.

As new technologies open up opportunities for collaboration and media production that are cheaper, easier and more accessible than ever, and as the Common Core State Standards (CCSS) spread across the US, now is the time for educators to explore the transformative potential of critical media literacy (CML). Current pressures for standardization, privatization, and high-stakes testing are driving public education to focus more on global competition than on democratic ideals and social justice. In this book, we propose that CML ped-agogy is an important strategy for educators to strengthen civic engagement and reassert the promise of democracy with an informed and empowered cit-izenry. We explore key theoretical discourses and discuss how a CML peda-gogy can be put into practice and included in teacher education programs so that pre-service teachers are better prepared to guide their students in critical inquiry *with* and *about* information communication technologies (ICTs) and popular culture.

As Freire (2010), Zinn (2005), and many others assert, recognizing the political nature of education and literacy is essential for transformative teaching and democracy. CML is a pedagogy that guides teachers and students to think critically about the world around them; it empowers them to act as responsible citizens, with the skills and social consciousness to challenge injustice. The development of CML highlights core concepts from cultural studies, critical theory, and new digital literacies (boyd, 2014; Ferguson, 2004; Hall, 1998; Kellner, 1995; Masterman, 2001; Morrell, 2012). It also provides a framework that encourages people to read information critically in multiple formats, to create alternative representations that question hierarchies of power, social norms and injustices, and to become agents of change.

Technology's exponential growth, as well as the convergence of media corporations and new media platforms, are changing society and students to be more mediated and networked than ever (Jenkins, 2006; McChesney, 2015; Prensky, 2010). Facebook, created in 2004, already reports one fifth of the world's population as active users, 1.47 billion of whom use it daily (Facebook, 2018). Even though Facebook is no longer the most popular social media platform for most US teens, replaced by Snapchat and Instagram (PEW, 2018), it is still one of the largest corporations in the world. Millions of youth walk into their classrooms with pocket-sized devices that provide immediate access to information and entertainment as well as the potential to create and disseminate multimedia messages that can travel the world in seconds.

CML offers students and educators an opportunity to rethink teaching and learning as political acts of consciousness raising and empowerment. While the CCSS has some significant problems (Brady, 2012), it can also be a tool to support educators in moving toward a more critical approach to incorporating literacy across all subjects and encouraging students to participate in their learning *with* and *about* digital media. The CCSS's call for more use of media and technology in the classrooms should be qualified with the point that *more* use of media and technology does not necessarily improve learning. Moreover, media and technology are not neutral tools. Rather, they are themselves embedded within socio-political contexts, as Stoddard (2014) explains:

> Too often, the connection of servers and millions of miles of fiber-optic cables that are the hardware and guts of the Internet are viewed as neutral and free of control. This assumption of neutrality overlooks the many people and software (created by people) that are central to the creation,

translation, and routing of information along these fibers or eventually through the air on satellite, Wi-Fi, or cellular networks. (p. 1)

The attention of the ccss to media and technology is movement in the right direction (Moore & Bonilla, 2014), but in order for these new tools to serve the goals of a responsible participative democracy, media and technology should be used within a cml framework.

New Technologies/New Literacies

Traditional ideas of literacy that focus on a standard national language and phonetic decoding are no longer sufficient in an age of countless communication systems and increasing linguistic and cultural diversity (New London Group, 1996). The traditional model of reading and writing is a positivist psychological model that frames literacy as individual cognitive skills that attempt to discover a fixed external reality. This paradigm needs to evolve to a deeper sociological understanding of literacy as a social practice with multiple perspectives "tied up in the politics and power relations of everyday life in literate cultures" (Luke & Freebody, 1997, p. 185). Lewis and Jhally (1998) express their concern "that media education in the United States will flounder if it cannot locate media texts in a broad set of social realities" (p. 3). They argue that when media literacy focuses on the text at the expense of the context, it ignores important questions of ideology, power, political economy, production, and reception. Lewis and Jhally do not suggest replacing a text-centered approach with a contextual approach, but like Luke and Freebody (1997), they call for including a sociological perspective with the psychological and cognitive ideas that are most common in literacy education. This type of reading and writing beyond the text is also a key component of the *Four Resources Model* (Luke & Freebody, 1999). Emerging from their work in Australia, the Four Resources Model lists four competences that are necessary for being literate in a multimodal world: breaking the code of texts, participating in the meanings of text, using texts functionally, and critically analyzing and transforming the texts (Luke & Freebody, 1999). As Vasquez (2003) explains:

> Luke and Freebody assert that reading should be seen as a nonneutral form of cultural practice, one that positions readers in advantageous and disadvantageous ways. They argue that readers need to be able to interrogate the assumptions and ideologies that are embedded in a text as well as the assumptions that they, as sociocultural beings, bring to the

text. This leads to asking questions such as, Whose voice is heard? Who is silenced? Whose reality is presented? Whose reality is ignored? Who is advantaged? Who is disadvantaged? These sorts of questions open spaces for analyzing the discourses or ways of being that maintain certain social practices over others. (p. 15)

Utilizing The Four Resources Model as a lens to analyze technology in the CCSS, Pandya and Aukerman (2014) illuminate the lack of critical competencies in the language of the new standards. They describe critical competencies relating to technology as: "The ability to critique and analyze texts, and to redesign new print and digital texts (sometimes as part of that critique); the knowledge that texts are never neutral but always embody particular points of view" (p. 429). Pandya and Aukerman (2014) caution that if teachers do not provide specific attention "to building children's *critical competencies,* we suspect that both children and teachers will remain focused on interpreting, creating, and sharing (digital) texts at the expense of analyzing and critiquing the power relations that underlie and are formed by texts" (p. 432). Students today need the skills and disposition to engage with messages in multiple ways, especially if they are to play a role in shaping democracy. This sociological understanding of literacy can be linked to a transformative pedagogy and media education that critiques the dominant ideologies of gender, race, and class through a contextual approach. It addresses the ideological frameworks and how they operate in the cultural milieu that collectively shapes and is shaped by media and the people who engage with them. This pedagogy aims to explore complex relationships among audiences, information, entertainment, power, and ideology.

Media, Power, and Ideology

Amid the struggles for bourgeois democracy in Europe during the 1848 revolutions, Karl Marx and Friedrich Engels (1978) developed a critical approach to ideology. According to Marx and Engels, ideologies arise from "dominant material relations expressed as ideas; hence of the relations which make the one class the ruling one, therefore, the ideas of its dominance" (Durham & Kellner, 2006, p. 44). For Marx, the emerging dominant class was the bourgeoisie and its dominant beliefs legitimated a capitalist market system with its ideas of free self-regulating markets, competition, and individualism, concepts that remain dominant in capitalist societies today.

Ideologies have social dimensions and are not simply individual perspectives that compete on a level playing field (Ferguson, 2004; Orlowski, 2006).

Durham and Kellner (2006) explain that studying ideology encourages "readers to perceive that all cultural texts have distinct biases, interests, and embedded values, reproducing the point of view of their producers and often the values of the dominant social groups" (p. xiv). By examining their ideological assumptions, students can learn to question what they consider "normal," or "common sense." The assumption that something is "common sense" is only so because ideas and texts have been produced and disseminated through a dominant frame of thought expressed in powerful master-narratives, often conveyed through media, schools, government, religion, or families.

Building upon Marx, from the 1930s through the 1960s, researchers at the Frankfurt Institute for Social Research (The Frankfurt School, i.e. Adorno, Benjamin, Habermas, Horkheimer, and Marcuse) saw the rise of popular culture through media as a process involving ideological message transmission vis à vis the culture industries, whereby film, radio, newspapers, and other organs of communication and culture transmit the dominant ideas of their society. They used critical social theory to analyze how popular culture and the new forms of communication technology perpetuated ideology and social control. The Frankfurt group immigrated to New York in 1934 as refugees from German fascism, where they had experienced how the Nazis used film, radio, and other media to transmit their fascist and totalitarian ideology (Kellner, 1989, 1995). Additionally, the German theorists studied Soviet Communism, examining how the Soviet state used the media to transmit dominant communist ideologies. While in the United States, they concluded that US popular culture and media transmitted dominant American and capitalist ideologies.

Frankfurt school theorists assumed that the audience is passive in its reception of media messages – a view that was challenged by a group of scholars in Birmingham, England, who advanced a more complex understanding of the active role audiences play in negotiating meanings. This group at the Centre for Contemporary Cultural Studies at the University of Birmingham (The Birmingham School created in 1964, i.e. Williams, Hoggart, and Hall), began to emphasize the role of the audience as active, rather than passive, in media reception (or consumption). Moreover, as women and scholars of color, including McRobbie and Gilroy, joined the group in the 1980s, they urged that the concept of ideology be expanded to include representations of gender, race, and sexuality, because media representations included sexist, racist and homophobic images and narratives that reproduce ideologies of patriarchal, racist, and heterosexist domination (Kellner, 1995, 2010). The Birmingham scholars also recognized that individuals experience and interpret media from their own class, gender, racial, and other positions, and can potentially resist and oppose classist, sexist, and racist ideologies. While the image of the media

audience as consumer became pervasive following the rise of audience theory studies, scholars have since heavily criticized the field for discounting the
heterogeneous ways in which viewers/listeners/users read, consume, or integrate media meaning into their lives (Buckingham, 1993, 1996; Gauntlett & Hill,
1999).

Understanding the role of context is an essential part of reading and writing the world and the word. When a text (whether it involves printed words,
an image, video, song, or T-shirt) is taken out of context, re-presented and/or
remixed, understandings of its message will vary because of the different contexts that readers bring with them, their prior knowledge, beliefs and experiences. Moreover, the contexts of how the message is constructed, the politics of
representation (the subjectivities of the people constructing the message, the
bias of those sharing the information), the qualities of the medium through
which the information is distributed, and the codes and conventions of the
text likewise have influence. Context is highly important and always influences
messages, regardless of whether listeners/readers/viewers are aware of it. No
message can be neutral, and no technology can represent information without
in some way affecting the message (McLuhan, 2003). Therefore, skills students
need to make sense of any information include the ability to question the construction and context of a text. This is the same challenge for determining the
bias of news reports and the accuracy of Internet postings. This task can be
more difficult when information is taken out of context, as is often the case in
mediated and networked publics where information is often shared, sampled,
and "mashed up." boyd (2014) emphasizes that in networked publics, contexts
are collapsed, thereby separating necessary details and merging disconnected
information, causing meaning making (comprehension) to become more
complicated. When a message is taken out of context, as is often the case with
social media, one's ability to communicate is challenged.

While media education has evolved from many disciplines, an important
arena of theoretical work for CML comes from the multidisciplinary field of
cultural studies. This is a field of critical inquiry comprised of the work of
researchers from The Frankfurt School, Birmingham School, feminism, queer
theory, critical race theory, critical indigenous theory, and others working to
examine the impact of the culture industries. These scholars have expanded
the concept of ideology to include gender, race, sexuality, and other forces of
identity and oppression in addition to class, while advancing a sophisticated
understanding of the audience as active makers of meaning. Applying concepts of semiotics, feminism, multiculturalism, postmodernism, a dialectical
understanding of political economy, textual analysis and audience theory, CML
has evolved into a practice of analyzing media and popular culture as dynamic

discourses that reproduce dominant ideologies as well as entertain, educate, and offer possibilities for counter-hegemonic alternatives.

In the 1980s, Cultural Studies research began to enter the educational arena. After the publication of Len Masterman's *Teaching the Media* (1985), many educators around the world embraced media education as a framework of *conceptual understandings* (Buckingham, 2003). While various media literacy organizations have their own list of essential ideas, most tend to coincide with at least five basic elements: (1) recognition of the construction of media and communication as a social process as opposed to accepting texts as isolated neutral or transparent conveyors of information; (2) textual analysis of the languages, genres, codes, and conventions of the text; (3) exploration of the role audiences play in negotiating meanings; (4) problematization of the process of representation to uncover and engage issues of ideology, power, and pleasure; (5) examination of the production and institutions that motivate and structure the media industries as corporate profit-seeking businesses.

Unfortunately, much of the current literature on media education in the US tends to marginalize CML as an outlier or label it as protectionist (Grieco, 2012; Hobbs, 2013), without recognizing that the core concepts of media literacy evolved from critical traditions and frameworks. Masterman's (1985) foundational text devotes an entire chapter to ideology and stresses the importance of media education to question hegemony and dominant myths. Masterman (1985) writes, "What must be kept absolutely clear, however, is the fact that the objectives of media education are demystificatory and critical" (p. 9). Perhaps one reason for the marginalization of CML is its focus on criticality.

The term "critical" is sometimes conflated with a negative judgment or an accusatory perspective. hooks (2010) explains, "there is a useful distinction to be made between critique that seeks to expand consciousness and harsh criticism that attacks or trashes" (p. 137). CML defines "critical" as an aspect of a dialectical, sociocultural, and analytical process. Campbell, Jensen, Gomery, Fabos, and Frechette (2013) assert, "Rather than cynically dismissing entire media styles and practices, the critical approach attempts to understand the institutional and interpretive processes through which media are made, distributed, and interpreted" (p. 8). This attempt at understanding invokes critical thinking that is more than just a cognitive idea; it is also a sociocultural understanding that seeks to develop in students a social consciousness as well as a working knowledge of how media operate. This notion of criticality is intended to develop the Freirian (2010) idea of "conscientizacao" (critical consciousness), a humanist liberatory understanding of living in solidarity with the world. Students are encouraged to question hegemony and social injustices in ways that can challenge problematic dominant narratives with their own counter-narratives as a form of praxis (reflection and action). As CML plays a vital role in addressing issues of social justice, it offers critical competencies for unveiling the social construction of normality and various forms of oppression and resistance.

As highlighted by Masterman in 1985, media can develop an ideological perspective through which their "facts" (and fiction) seem "normal." Masterman (1985) asserts that the media "carry out what is perhaps their most important ideological role through a process which is generally regarded as being ideologically innocent, the process of reporting 'the facts'" (p. 129). He suggests that educators should not only foster students' critical thinking skills to expose underlying media messages, but they should also facilitate the conversations that question ideological frames, or what makes information seem "normal." It is this examination of the social construction of ideologies that we explore in the next chapter.

CHAPTER 2

Ideology and the Politics of Representation

Critical media literacy is more difficult to understand and teach than most mainstream approaches to media education because of the complexity and invisibility of how ideology functions. Robert Ferguson (1998) states, "'Ideology' is not directly visible, but can only be experienced and/or comprehended. What is visible is a range of social and representational manifestations which are rooted in relationships of power and subordination" (p. 43). Through the process of *naturalizing* (making ideas *seem* "natural" or "normal") power relations, ideology removes from view their social and historical construction. What one does not see, one rarely questions. Therefore, progressive educators should guide students to ask critical questions that will help reveal the structures, history, and social contexts that are too often obscured from view by ideological hegemony.

As Stuart Hall (2003), one of the founders of British Cultural Studies argues, "ideology functions through "common sense" assumptions about what is considered "normal" as compared to all else that becomes the "other." The ideological discourse of "normality" is constructed through "othering" all that is not the "norm." It is in this context that Ferguson states, "The invocation of normality and the establishment of culturally and politically acceptable behavioural patterns often form the keystone for ideological arguments made at the expense of individuals, groups, or nations deemed to be 'other'" (p. 154). Hall (2003) further explains, "Ideologies tend to disappear from view into the taken-for-granted 'naturalised' world of common sense. Since (like gender) race appears to be 'given' by Nature, racism is one of the most profoundly 'naturalised' of existing ideologies" (p. 90). Ferguson in turn (1998), suggests that one reason race is such an important issue for media educators is

> because most of the information about "others" and "race" is available only through the mass media, the international or global dimension of representing 'race' is even more problematic than that which is concerned with local or regional affairs. Images of issues of "race" are likely to be multiple, fragmented and transitory. (p. 253)

Understanding the connections between the media and race is important because, as multicultural educator James Banks (2000) asserts, "The representation of people and groups in the media is a cogent factor that influences

© KONINKLIJKE BRILL NV, LEIDEN, 2019 | DOI: 10.1163/9789004404533_002

children's perceptions, attitudes, and values" (p. xiii). This influence of media on children has created a "media multicultural curriculum" that, according to Carlos Cortés (2000), denies educators "the power to decide *if* multicultural education will occur. It will...through the media, even if not in schools" (p. xvi). Cortés promotes a brand of media literacy that prioritizes multiculturalism to help students distinguish between generalizations and stereotypes. He writes that the mass media multicultural curriculum does not *cause* racism but it does *contribute* "significantly to the corpus of American thinking, feeling, and acting in the realm of diversity" (p. 69). Cortés suggests that the power of media to influence children's notions of "the Other" comes from the "frequency and variety" of representations (p. 154) of subordinate groups defined by race, ethnicity, class, gender and sexuality who appear as "other" and "inferior" to the dominant groups. According to Ferguson (1998), the most common representations of race tend to concentrate on individual figures more than social formations, thereby softening the "systematic processes of historical racism" (p. 218). Ferguson suggests that a historical perspective is important because it helps to see race not as natural or arbitrary, but rather as an ideological construction.

Intersectionality

Because of the multifaceted nature of media and popular culture, critical media literacy educators need to use a variety of theories and perspectives to engage meaningfully in the politics of representation. A multiperspectival approach deploys multiple forms of critical theories to examine the ways media texts represent identity and perpetuate discrimination (Kellner, 1995). The concept of *intersectionality* articulated by Kimberlé Crenshaw (1991) provides a powerful lens to uncover the intersections of oppression and domination across lines of class, race, gender, and other forms of oppression. This concept suggests that forms of oppression intersect and work together. Cultural theorists have used intersectionality to explore how representations of various identity markers such as race, class, and gender, intersect and create multiple sources of disempowerment. A critical cultural studies is also concerned with exploring representations that counter forms of oppression through depictions of struggle and emancipation in the contested terrain of contemporary media culture.

Patricia Hill Collins (2000) asserts, "An increasingly important dimension of why hegemonic ideologies concerning race, class, gender, sexuality, and nation remain so deeply entrenched lies, in part, in the growing sophistication of mass media in regulating intersecting oppressions" (p. 284). She states that dominant representations of Black women in media are often controlling images that objectify and subordinate. Collins writes, "Portraying African-American women as stereotypical mammies, matriarchs, welfare recipients, and hot mommas helps justify US Black women's oppression" (p. 69). Even though the specific images and stereotypes may change, Collins insists, "the overall ideology of domination itself seems to be an enduring feature of intersecting oppressions" (p. 88).

CML deploys a variety of theories and perspectives to engage a full range of the politics of representation in which media texts present constructs of class, race, gender, sexuality, and other constituents of identity in ways that promote oppression and perpetuate classism, racism, sexism, heterosexism and other forms of discrimination. The concept of *theory* derives from the Greek word *theoria* and denotes *a way of seeing* phenomena in the world. Each theory has its focuses and blind spots, so that a Marxist theory will focus on class, capitalism, economic themes, and ideology critique, while a Weberian analysis focuses on state, bureaucracy, and more political-institutional issues and processes. Classical feminist theory will focus intensely on gender and gender relations, critiquing sexist and patriarchal representations and narratives. Critical race theory engages constructions of race and ethnicity and critiques racism and racial stereotypes, while seeking representations that break with conventional limited and biased representations. Lesbian, Gay, Bisexual, Transgender, Queer/Questioning (LGBTQ) theories take on issues of gender and sexuality, critiquing heterosexism, homophobia, transphobia, and seeking more positive and diverse images of gender and sexuality. All of these theories thus have strong focuses and emphases, but also blind spots. Taken together, these theories and others constitute a powerful repertoire to engage the politics of representation as a contested terrain.

To be sure, some varieties of Marxism, feminism, and other critical theories adopt an intersectional approach, while CML proposes utilizing all relevant critical theories of the contemporary era that emerged during periods of social struggle over the past decades. Theories in this conception are ways of seeing that can engage the constellation of representations in a text concerning different identity markers and other dimensions of the *politics of representation*, which describes how media texts represent different social groups and dimensions of social existence. Theories can also provide *modes of interpretation* that can delineate the meanings, politics, and effects of texts in specific socio-historical contexts.

Standpoint Epistemologies

From studying the ideological structures of patriarchy, many feminist theorists like Patricia Hill-Collins developed feminist standpoint epistemologies
(Harding, 2004) that can be useful for critical media literacy. Privileges and
dominance create blind spots making it more difficult for those benefiting
from oppression to see the structures and ideologies that oppress others. At
the same time, people with less privileges who have lived and experienced the
effects of racism, sexism, classism, and other systemic forms of oppression are
more likely to recognize the problems and be able to see the harmful structures.
Standpoint theory is about studying up, beginning inquiry from marginalized
positions in order to increase the likelihood of seeing the larger social structures that often become obscured by hegemonic ideologies. While people who
experience oppression have greater potential for recognizing the structures of
oppression, critical consciousness is not automatic. Feminist standpoint theorists assert, "the vision available to the oppressed group must be struggled
for..." (Hartsock, 1997, p. 153).

Since most research and media reports start their inquiries from dominant
positions (like TV war coverage that first interview military officials before
talking with civilian casualties), standpoint theorists argue for the need to
reverse the starting place and begin with the people most affected by the
oppressive structures and systems. Changing the location of where one begins
their research increases the odds of accessing experiences and insights that are
often missing from the dominant discourse. It also tends to reduce the blind
spots and smoke screens of ideologies that "naturalize" and "normalize" social
constructions as "common-sense."

Critical media literacy that combines critical pedagogy with standpoint
epistemologies can offer an approach to help all students see the structures
of oppression, analyze the role of ideology in shrouding those structures, and
find agency in the act of becoming subjects who can express their voices to
challenge racism, sexism, classism, and all forms of oppression. Creating alternative media and coming to voice is important for everyone, especially people
who have seldom been allowed to speak for themselves, but without critical
analysis, it is not enough. Critical analysis that explores and exposes the structures of oppression is essential because merely coming to voice is something
any marginalized racist or sexist group of people can also claim. Spaces must
be opened and opportunities created so that people in marginalized positions have the opportunity to collectively struggle against oppression to voice
their concerns and create their own alternative representations. This process
can also help students in dominant positions recognize their blind spots and

become more sensitive to the systems of oppression from which they are benefiting. By changing the starting point of inquiry, from top down to bottom up, the potential is greater for everyone to build a critical consciousness that can empathize with the oppressed and pierce through the ideological hegemony to see the institutions and systems that dominate.

Questioning Power

Through group discussions, critical analysis, and political struggle, classrooms can be transformed into pedagogical spaces of liberation (Freire, 2010), and not simply social reproduction. Marginalized voices and alternative perspectives offer great potential to challenge dominant discourse by exposing the myth that information and knowledge can be objective and separate from power. Michel Foucault (1995) writes, "there is no power relation without the correlative constitution of a field of knowledge, nor any knowledge that does not presuppose and constitute at the same time power relations" (p. 27). Since people with desires, fears, and prejudices construct ideas within social and historical contexts, there is no information or knowledge that is ever objective or neutral. Sandra Harding (2004) explains, "The more value-neutral a conceptual framework appears, the more likely it is to advance the hegemonic interests of dominant groups, and less likely it is to be able to detect important actualities of social relations" (p. 6). A strategy for counteracting hegemony is exposing its construction and unveiling the biases inherent in all communication.

Freire's *problem-posing* education that encourages students to collectively engage with problems and then wrestle with solving them can fit well with standpoint theory and critical media literacy. He reports, "cooperation leads dialogical Subjects to focus their attention on the reality which mediates them and which – posed as a problem – challenges them. The response to that challenge is the action of dialogical Subjects upon reality in order to transform it" (1970, p. 168). Feminist theorist Jane Flax (1997) suggests that with critical feminism, "'reality' will appear even more unstable, complex, and disorderly than it does now" (p. 178). It is through problematizing reality that knowledge and stories from marginalized positions can have much greater potential to demystify hegemony and offer alternative epistemologies. When aiming for social transformation, students should begin inquiry from marginal positions and then study up as part of the process of collective political struggle. While this may sound too radical for public education, it is actually in line with the basic principles of democracy and the US Bill of Rights. Democracy and liberty require a type of literacy that goes far beyond the mere ability to read and write. Henry Giroux (1987) states, "To be literate is *not* to be free, it is to be present and active in the struggle for reclaiming one's voice, history, and future" (p. 11).

If students learn to deconstruct and reconstruct media with a critical media literacy framework and through a standpoint methodology, they increase their ability to recognize hegemonic myths, deepen their understanding of structural oppression, and expand their empathic capacity to act in solidarity with those struggling for their rights. The first conceptual understanding of critical media literacy asserts, "all information is co-constructed by individuals and/or groups of people who make choices within social contexts." Harding (1998) uses the term *co-constructivism*:

> to emphasize how systematic knowledge-seeking is always just one element in any culture, society, or social formation in its local environment, shifting and transforming other elements – education systems, legal systems, economic relations, religious beliefs and practices, state projects (such as war-making), gender relations – as it, in turn, is transformed by them. (p. 4)

This description of co-constructivism can be useful to demythologize the social construction process and at the same time expose the interconnectedness of people, ideas, and society. Harding (1998) explains, "We can retain the best of both realist and constructivist understandings of the relations between our social worlds, our representations, and the realities our representations are intended to represent by thinking of co-evolving, or co-constructing, cultures and their knowledge projects" (p. 20).

Understanding these interconnections and interdependence is necessary, according to Ferguson (2001), to create *critical solidarity*. He suggests that our relationships with media are not autonomous, but rather they depend on taking positions related to social contexts. Since we are always taking sides, Ferguson (2001) calls for critical solidarity as "a means by which we acknowledge the social dimensions of our thinking and analysis. It is also a means through which we may develop our skills of analysis and relative autonomy" (p. 42). Critical solidarity means teaching students to interpret information and communication within humanistic, social, historical, political, and economic contexts for them to understand the interrelationships and consequences of their actions and lifestyles. It also means joining in solidarity with the disempowered in a collective struggle for a more just world.

At this point, when ideas about media education are being taken up around the world, it is imperative that critical pedagogy be a central component.

Critical media literacy should be built upon a solid foundation that applies ideas from Dewey's experiential education and Freire's problem-posing pedagogy. These educational theories require learning to begin with what students already know, building on their experiences, confronting the problems they encounter in their daily lives, and helping them to express their ideas and concerns to audiences beyond the classroom. Student-centered education should spiral out into new areas of learning as students explore and search for meanings. When the goal of critical solidarity guides media education, students can work together to unveil and demythologize their media.

Contemporary societies differentiate people along the axis of class, gender, race, sexuality, ability, religion, and other identity markers. Throughout this book we engage with the way media images and narratives legitimate the dominant class, race, and gender positions and reproduce racism, classism, sexism, homophobia, and other forms of discrimination and oppression. We begin with engaging representations of class and classism in media since there are fewer studies and discussions of this dimension than the growing literature on representations of race, gender, and sexuality – all of which are crucial dimensions of a critical media literacy.

Representations of Class Divisions

Commercial media in the US too often tell stories that celebrate lifestyles of over-consumption and wealth, while neglecting narratives of the working class and poor. When media address issues of class, they typically denigrate the poor as dangerous or lazy, ignoring the social structures and institutions that perpetuate social and economic disparity. Class divisions and structural inequalities have long been powerful systems organizing society and controlling people's lives. Since enormous transnational corporations control so much of the information and entertainment, the stories they tell about class need to be deconstructed, analyzed, challenged, and reconstructed. It is because of the power of media culture to construct the narratives and position audiences about our understandings of socioeconomics that critical media literacy must address issues of class and the ways it intersects with all aspects of our lives.

A CML approach to teaching about socioeconomic status (SES) reminds educators and students that the questions that need to be asked are often the ones that challenge what some consider to be the most fundamental building blocks of society. Critical pedagogues like Michael Apple (2004), Freire (2010), Henry Giroux (2004), and bell hooks (2010) address inequities of class in education. While a dominant ideology holds that class is disappearing in contemporary US society, in fact class distinctions are growing, especially in relation to race. In a report that focuses on US wealth rather than income inequality, the authors assert, "We find that without a serious change in course, the country is heading towards a racial and economic apartheid state" (Asante-Muhammad, Collins, Hoxie, & Nieves, 2017, p. 3).

Hence, while ideologues of contemporary society claim that great inequalities of class have been overcome, this is simply false, as scholars such as Atkinson (2010) and Piketty (2014) have maintained. On the whole, dominant media, like film and television, often celebrate the rich and powerful while negatively representing poor and working people. Traditionally, US television focused on middle class families, professionals like doctors, lawyers, or corporate executives, while tending to ignore working class life. Based on over four decades studying TV portrayals of class on US prime-time sitcoms, Richard Butsch (2003) reports persistent patterns of underrepresentation of working-class occupations and negative stereotypes of working-class men. Butsch asserts that these representations work well to "justify class relations of modern capitalism" (p. 575). To be sure, some TV series like *The Honeymooners, All in the Family, Sanford and Son, Roseanne, Shameless, Superstore,* and *One Day at a Time* have shown problems and conflicts within working-class life in sympathetic ways, as do some contemporary Hollywood films. While the growth of cable networks and the Internet has depicted more diversity, the majority of representations still valorize the wealthy at the expense of the working-class and poor. Although the entire media landscape should never be overly simplified as monolithic and one-dimensional in its portrayal of social class issues, it continues to favor a model of economic success grounded in dogged individualism detached from larger social structures or communities of subjugation, mutual support, and struggle.

Typically in the US, class is rarely discussed, and we are often told that we live in a classless society where everyone is in the middle class. And yet the dominant ideology of the "American Dream" proclaims that with hard work (and education) anyone can move up the socioeconomic ladder and achieve their dreams and highest aspirations. To be sure, many people in the US, through education, intersecting privileges, and good fortune, have been able to advance themselves, but not everyone. The gaps between different classes and the tremendous inequality between the rich and poor makes it extremely difficult, if not impossible, for many to leave poverty and to gain wealth and a more privileged class status. Yet, as promulgated by popular media like young adult novels in the 1800s, the Horatio Alger myth persists, suggesting that anyone can rise from rags-to-riches if they just work hard enough.

Whereas European societies have traditionally been organized around class and its configuration, constraints, and social relations are visible and well-known to all in the society, in the United States, class is hard to see. Indeed, class is almost invisible unless you know where to look and what to look for. Social class is heavily coded, with specific words and images connoting many notions and often triggering demeaning stereotypes about the poor and working class, and belief in class supremacy in the upper classes. Many words have class connotations, like welfare, White trash, trailer park, homeless, and beggar, which hold negative associations. There is much deficit thinking (Valencia, 1997) about class, and often in political, social, and media discourses, members of the underclass are blamed for being poor, in terms of deficits of education, upbringing, job training, and opportunities to better themselves, which are a product of social organization and not inherent or inherited traits of human nature. When personal traits are mentioned, the poor are often judged through a meritocratic lens that disparages them for not trying hard enough and lacking "grit." This deficit thinking implies that if they just tried harder and persevered, then they could be anything they want, with no recognition of social inequities and systematic structures of oppression.

In England, spoken accent has long been a marker for class, as in the movie *My Fair Lady*, and good teeth can mark class in images and discourses in the US. For example, a December 1, 1997, issue of *Newsweek* Magazine manipulated a photo on their cover to make a woman's teeth look better. The *Newsweek* cover photo shows Bobbi McCaughey, mother of septuplets, with straight teeth. The same week, *Time* Magazine ran a similar photo without manipulating the mother's teeth. The photoshopping of the mother's teeth seems to suggest that *Newsweek* did not want a woman on their cover who looked poor, and provided a normative image of the "proper" American that subtly inscribes class markers.

Critical media literacy makes one aware of how images in media construct markers, hierarchies, and relations of class in contemporary society. The concept of intersectionality (Crenshaw, 1991) indicates how class, gender, race, and sexuality intersect and are co-constructed. For instance, media narratives that portray class often have images and thematics involving gender, race, and sexuality, so that a CML that critiques racism, sexism, and homophobia, also critiques classism. CML also explores how media images portray positive, negative, or sometimes ambiguous images and messages about certain social classes, for example, denigrating the working classes and celebrating the rich or middle class. Yet, just as criticizing biased representations of class is an important dimension of CML, so too is explicating and validating media texts that present positive images of the working class, women, people of color, LGBTQ individuals, and others who are often represented negatively in mainstream media. As the concept of intersectionality suggests, these representations often overlap and intersect, thus offering complex and productive examinations in the classroom.

In 2011, the Occupy Movement foregrounded the class divide between the 1% and the 99%, and class division and inequality entered public discourse. In addition, Bernie Sanders' 2016 campaign for president created a powerful social movement focusing on the gap between rich and poor, the haves and have-nots, and the need for dramatic political change and action to address class and other forms of inequality in the US.

Courses in CML can analyze a variety of ways in which media represent class, for example, questioning media representations of gentrification as a positive improvement and poverty as a negative condition. CML can discuss how capitalism constructs class and divides societies into working classes and property owning classes, with a vast middle class in-between. CML guides us to engage a political system that often operates in the interests of the wealthier classes, while criticizing programs for the poor that do not enable them to escape the chains of poverty. Or students could discuss how some political groups do not want to provide any but the most minimal social welfare programs.

CML should also question the connections between class and the environment, health, and social justice, showing how living and working conditions affect poor people far worse than wealthier groups, linking environmental and class issues. Naomi Klein (2014) writes about environmental justice in her book, *This Changes Everything: Capitalism vs the Climate*, bringing together discussion of class, economics, environmental crisis and exploitation. In short, a CML approach to teaching, questions the connections between power and information, class and education. In a capitalist society, this requires posing questions that challenge social class, and unpack the economic structures that are often taken for granted.

Looking Closely at Race and Racism

As we explore the politics of representation, we need to address issues of race and racism in media because "race has been a master category, a kind of template for patterns of inequality, marginalization, and difference throughout U.S. history" (Omi & Winant, 2015, p. viii). The history of racism in the US has had devastating effects and continues today by normalizing American identity as White; thereby marginalizing other racial identities, dividing the country along the "color line," and contributing to ideological and structural systems that benefit Whites while disadvantaging people of color. Robert Ferguson (1998) asserts that the importance of a historic perspective is to avoid seeing race as "arbitrary or 'natural'" (p. 78). Since Europeans arrived in North America, racial discrimination has been used to decimate Native Americans (through murder, theft, and genocide) and justify kidnapping and enslaving human beings from various parts of the world, especially Africa. White Americans and the US economy have benefited greatly from taking native lands and exploiting slave labor.

The actions, policies, and laws that have long privileged Whites at the expense of people of color have continued throughout US history. Yale law professor James Whitman (2017) writes:

> In the early twentieth century the United States was not just a country with racism. It was *the* leading racist jurisdiction – so much so that even Nazi Germany looked to America for inspiration…the United States, with its deeply rooted white supremacy and its vibrant and innovative legal culture, was the country at the forefront of the creation of racist law. (p. 138)

Whitman documents how the Nazi Nuremberg Laws were heavily influenced by American racist laws and policies such as: Jim Crow segregation (voting laws and legal segregation), immigration, naturalization, and citizenship laws, second class citizenship status, anti-miscegenation laws, American eugenics movement, and American lynch justice.

Up until the early 1900s, biology and religion were the dominant paradigms for understanding race in the US. However, following World War I, a new approach to understanding race emerged that focused on culture and ethnicity and saw race as a social construction. This move to a sociological race/ethnicity paradigm was an improvement from the previous ideas that assumed race was based on genetics or an act of god. Yet, the ethnicity paradigm's focus on assimilation and cultural pluralism lacks essential elements of race such as history, the body (the ocular dimension), economics, and social structures (Omi & Winant, 2015). This notion of ethnicity also tends to universalize Whiteness as the norm for all other ethnicities to assimilate into. As the civil rights movements grew in the 1960s, Black Power, Chican@ Power, and other groups pushed for a deeper understanding of race and racism. With these moves, dominant racial projects appropriated and shifted the ethnicity approach to the right, and by the 1970s, the race/ethnicity paradigm became a neoconservative way of promoting the hegemony of colorblindness. It is the combination of ideological and structural realities of race and racism that create the racial projects shaping race relations in the US, thereby maintaining the color line. Michael Omi and Howard Winant (2015) write:

> We conceive of racial formation processes as occurring through a linkage between structure and signification. *Racial projects* do both the ideological and the practical "work" of making these links and articulating the connections between them. *A racial project is simultaneously an interpretation, representation, or explanation of racial identities and meanings, and an effort to organize and distribute resources (economic, political, cultural) along particular racial lines.* (p. 125)

Throughout the history of American film, broadcasting, and television there has been a tradition of racist representations of people of color, from *The Birth of a Nation* (D.W. Griffith, 1914) which celebrated the Ku Klux Klan and presented pernicious stereotypical images of Blacks, to Hollywood genre films that present people of color as subordinate servants, or threatening criminals (see Benshoff & Griffin, 2009; Bogle, 1989; Fregoso, 1993; Shaheen, 2001). During the 2018 midterm elections, broadcast news, social media, and rightwing propaganda stoked feelings of fear by spreading fictitious claims that a caravan of migrants was bringing contagious diseases, "criminals and unknown Middle Easterners," to the US (Berr, 2018; Roose, 2018; Vernon, 2018). A commercial created by the Republican party about the caravan was deemed too racist by CNN to be aired, soon followed by NBC and Fox News who eventually pulled the ad after allowing it to be broadcast (https://tinyurl.com/yc3j7ffk).

The connection between racial representations and discriminatory social structures, reinforces the importance of critically analyzing media messages because the meaning of any text is never fixed or transparent. Stuart Hall (2013) explains that meaning "is a slippery customer, changing and shifting with context, usage and historical circumstances" (p. xxv). He asserts that meanings can cause us to feel powerful positive and negative emotions. "They sometimes call our very identities into question. We struggle over them because they matter – and these are contests from which serious consequences can flow. They define what is 'normal,' who belongs – and therefore, who is excluded. They are deeply inscribed in relations of power" (p. xxv). Hall (2013) states:

> since the "cultural turn" in the human and social sciences, meaning is thought to be *produced* – constructed – rather than simply "found." Consequently, in what has come to be called a "social constructionist approach," representation is conceived as entering into the very constitution of things; and thus culture is conceptualized as a primary or

"constitutive" process, as important as the economic or material "base" in shaping social subjects and historical events – not merely a reflection of the world after the event. (p. xxi)

The power of signification through media representations is especially challenging when exploring issues of race and racism because so much of the dominant ideology has normalized race as natural and biological, without historical, social, economic, or political context. In order to challenge this process, Ferguson (1998) proposes the concept of *productive unease*:

> Here the tendency has always been to naturalise relations of power and subordination in a manner which effaces the social origins of beliefs and judgements...the process of naturalising racist relations of power and subordination is still the key societal feature which needs to be undermined and eliminated. Denaturalisation of media representations refuses to accept everyday definitions and requires one to live in a state of what I call productive unease. (p. 6)

CML pedagogy can promote "productive unease" as students question the social construction of race and recognize the painful realities of racism through debunking the ideology of White supremacy and the false connection of race with biology. By invoking ideas from Afro-Media Literacy (Byard, 2012), educators can explore the connections between history, science, economics, and ideology with current portrayals of African Americans in media and popular culture. Developed by Shani Byard (2012), Afro-Media Literacy guides students to question the dominant structures that have for centuries shaped the way race and racism have been constructed in the US to benefit White European immigrants and their descendants at the expense of people of color, especially African Americans. Key points for discourse within the Afro-Media Literacy framework include: (1) analyzing *slavery* as a defining point for American racism, (2) recognizing the role of *eugenics* to justify racial hierarchies, (3) exploring the way *economics* exploits racism for profit and power, and (4) confronting *colorism* as a tool for promoting Black inferiority and White superiority.

The history of eugenics and scientific racism remains largely unknown to many students in the US, even though it still informs much popular discourse and many media messages such as the *New York Times* bestseller, *The Bell Curve* (Hernstein & Murray, 1994) and *A Troublesome Inheritance: Genes, Race and Human History* (Wade, 2014) written by a 30-year veteran *New York Times* science writer (Rendall, 2014). A recent critique of eugenics can be found in an excellent PBS *American Experience* documentary that aired on October 16, 2018, titled "The Eugenics Crusade: What's Wrong with Perfect?" (https://tinyurl.com/ycs9rpsq). This documentary could serve as a potent teaching-tool for high school and university classes.

These ideas of White superiority have been present in much mainstream media in the US for centuries and aspects of it continue today. It was only in 2018 that *National Geographic Magazine* admitted to its role in perpetuating racism through its reporting. The magazine's Editor in Chief Susan Goldberg (2018) writes, "It hurts to share the appalling stories from the magazine's past" but admits "how we present race matters" (p. 4). Since 1888, National Geographic magazine has been reinforcing racist colonial ideas through articles and pictures of people and cultures around the world. Goldberg explains that the magazine failed to report on social problems or share the voices of people of color, and instead "pictured 'natives' elsewhere as exotics, famously and frequently unclothed, happy hunters, noble savages – every type of cliché" (p. 4). One caption to a photograph from a story about Australia in 1916 reads: "South Australian Blackfellows: These savages rank lowest in intelligence of all human beings" (pp. 4–6). These repeated representations have contributed powerfully to the process of normalizing ideologies of White supremacy. Current media portrayals are often more subtle, yet continue to perpetuate these same ideas through many practices, such as labeling: Muslim mass shooters are "terrorists" and White mass shooters are "mentally ill" or "lone wolves"; Latin American immigrants are "criminals" while Eastern European immigrants are "refugees"; and unarmed African American protestors are "thugs" while White armed militiamen are "activists," even as they point automatic weapons at law enforcement (Pearce, Duara, & Yardley, 2016).

Stuart Hall (2003) explains that words and images can connote various meanings when they are articulated (connected) through ideological frameworks. Deficit thinking is one of the more common ideologies that suggests certain groups of people are deficient in positive characteristics, such as: honesty, intelligence, commitment to work hard, desire to improve their status, and grit. These assumptions of deficiencies, promote the idea that these people deserve their situation because of their own faults. Throughout US history, various racialized groups have been recipients of deficit thinking at different times, yet Native Americans and African Americans have continually suffered from these assertions often contributing to experiences of historical trauma (Arrows, 2013; DeGruy, 2005).

Commercial media often reproduce deficit thinking through framing poverty as the fault of the poor who are too lazy to work hard or unable to defer gratification. The dominant discourse around poverty in the US, especially when connected to people of color, has long blamed either a culture of poverty, inferior genes, or inadequate parents and home life (Valencia & Solórzano, 2004). The ideology of deficit thinking is used to justify inequality and injustice by blaming the victims of discrimination and racism for their inability to be successful, shifting the responsibility away from the institutions, structures, and systems of oppression. Educators can work to counteract deficit thinking by recognizing their own biases, examining the social structures that create inequality, and using an asset-based approach to validate their students' experiences, cultures, and *funds of knowledge* (González, Moll, & Amanti, 2005).

It is important to explore the social constructions of race from the past to better understand the current expressions of racism in the present, especially as popular discourse claims to have moved beyond race. The continuing racial disparity of opportunities, privileges, discriminatory practices, and microaggressions are now often less overt than in the past, however they are no less destructive to individuals and society. Decades of research by Claude Steele and his colleagues about "stereotype threats" provides empirical evidence of the destructive power that words, gestures, and signification can have on the human body. When people experience words or actions (cues) that suggest their marginality, a *stereotype threat* is likely to occur, causing anxiety, affecting physiology (sweating, hypertension, increased heart rate, higher blood pressure), and impairing cognitive thinking abilities (Steele, 2010). Steele conducted experiments in which researchers said comments to just certain subjects that would trigger negative stereotypes and then tested all the subjects and repeatedly found the subjects who were triggered would perform worse on the test. For example, Black students told that a test would measure intelligence, women reminded of their gender before taking a math test, or older people questioned about their ability to remember, all performed worse on the test after the mention of characteristics associated with a negative stereotype connected to their identity. The stereotype threat phenomenon demonstrates the power of stereotypes and the importance of analyzing and challenging outright racism as well as the more indirect microaggressions.

Racial Microaggressions were originally identified by Chester Pierce in the 1970s and have since been interpreted in various disciplines from Law to Education. Microaggressions are subtle, sometimes non-verbal, commonplace exchanges, that communicate negative messages to people in marginalized groups. The purpose of the microaggression can be negative with malice or positive with well-intentioned motives and unintended negative consequences. Therefore, it is important for educators to help students focus on the effects rather than the intent, because the negative effects of a microaggression are harmful, whether they were meant to be or not. Kiyun Kim

(2013) confronted racial microaggressions with an alternative media project she created at Fordham University. She photographed her classmates holding signs with actual racial microaggressions they have heard said about them, such as: "You're not really Asian," "Why do you sound White?", and "No, where are you REALLY from?" This collection of photographs went viral on the Internet and were reposted on numerous websites (see the collection at http://nortonism.tumblr.com/).

Microaggressions can be experienced in many ways from comments spoken, to representations omitted, to topics and people chosen to be remembered. James Lowen (1999) points out that the person with the most historical markers commemorating his legacy in any state is "Nathan Bedford Forrest, Confederate cavalry leader and founder of the Ku Klux Klan, in Tennessee" (p. 16). Recently, there have been numerous protests about Confederate symbols and statues on display in public areas; over 1,700 monuments and tributes to the Confederacy remain (Southern Poverty Law Center, 2018). These glorifications of the Civil War are for many people, painful reminders of the brutal history of slavery.

Similar experiences are felt by Native Americans when sports teams use mascots or names that belittle their culture. Since 1890, about 200 pioneer monuments have been erected in the US, mostly with just White people, but occasionally including a Native American at the bottom. Cynthia Prescott (2018) explains that these statues "explicitly celebrated the dominant white view of the Wild West progressing from American Indian 'savagery' to white 'civilization.'" These celebrations of White supremacy continue the legacy of racist policies, broken treaties, and misinformation campaigns that have provoked some of the worst atrocities in this country's history. Statues and monuments are media that should be interrogated within the CML framework like any other media text, especially in regards to the connections between information and power.

The power to determine what information and representations people will find in books, media, when they travel across the country, or search on the Internet are influential forces that shape ideas and can perpetuate dominant narratives. The rapid growth of search engines has changed the way people look for information and judge credibility; Google now answers about 3.5 billion searches every day. Scott Galloway (2017) writes, "Google is a modern man's god. It's our source of knowledge – ever-present, aware of our deepest secrets, reassuring us where we are and where we need to go, answering questions from trivial to profound. No institution has the trust and credibility of Google" (p. 5). Yet these search engines are neither public information utilities nor public spaces like libraries. Safiya Noble (2018) emphasizes that Google is an advertising company using invisible algorithms and PageRanked search protocols that have led to racist and sexist results in the name of profit. While searching online for information about the accomplishments and intellectual traditions of people like her young nieces and their friends, Noble typed the words, "black girls" into a Google search and was inundated with pornographic websites (Noble, 2012). This led her to investigate the biases of search engines and in 2018 publish her book, *Algorithms of Oppression: How Search Engines Reinforce Racism*. Noble asserts that it is a serious problem when most people consider search engines to be neutral tools for answering any question because when so many of our decision-making systems are automated by profit-seeking corporations, we need to question what values are prioritized, and at whose expense.

When considering the role teachers should play in the 21st century, Tyrone Howard (2010) asserts that all educators need to have a racial awareness "that recognizes the historical, social, political, and economic consequences of being a member of a racially marginalized group in the United States" (p. 121). He points out that racial awareness is more than simply acknowledging differences, "but consists of a consciousness of how race is manifested in the United States...Racial awareness also entails having a working knowledge of how 'Whiteness' permeates US ideologies, culture, and practices" (p. 121). These are issues that teachers and teacher educators need to explore in order to be able to engage in courageous conversations about race and racism with their students. As Howard (2010) explains it, "teacher educators should be willing to push students into the uncomfortable spaces where race is being discussed on an in-depth level" (p. 123). Indeed, if teachers do not feel prepared, they may "retreat to the safety net of practicing 'colorblindness,' the practice of not acknowledging the racial identities of their students" that often "renders students of color invisible" and makes Whiteness the norm (p. 123). Howard contends, "Colorblind perspectives also may contribute to internalized racism, reinforce racial hierarchies, and contribute to the development of deficit models about students of color" (p. 124).

Critical media literacy provides a framework for creating the "productive unease" necessary to have these courageous conversations about race and racism. Through questioning media representations of race and racism we can begin to unpack the way information and power function to benefit some at the expense of others.

Problematizing Gender and Sexuality

From the Judeo-Christian bible to the latest popular video game, patriarchal values continue to be part of the ideological foundation of contemporary commercial media. Indeed, the "common-sense" assumption that men should hold power over women because they are inherently stronger, smarter, and better is not universal, but it is a dominant contemporary social construction in many parts of the world, often thanks in part to media representations and cultural practices. The cultural dominance of patriarchy creates assumptions about the subordinate roles women are expected to play in relation to the privileged positions from which men benefit. CML questions how patriarchy and the domination of women are advanced or contested by media representations that often objectify women's bodies and disregard their minds.

Ideologies and structures of patriarchy and sexism intersect with heterosexism. When heterosexuality is represented as the "normal" way of understanding sexuality, romantic relationships are limited to those between men and women in movies, songs, and advertisements. As heterosexual romance and gender conformity are ubiquitous in media, they marginalize LGBTQ individuals and communities while reinforcing assumptions that heterosexuality is the only option. It is important to interrogate the social construction of gender and sexuality and the ways that media help co-construct our conceptions. Critical gender studies engage the role of media in the social construction of masculinities, femininities, and the various gender identities in relations of domination and subordination in a patriarchal, heterosexist society.

To begin unpacking the social construction of gender and sexuality, a helpful tool available online is the Genderbread Person (https://tinyurl.com/qxw7g7u) or the Gender Unicorn (http://www.transstudent.org/gender). These visual graphics illustrate differences between the categories: gender identity, gender expression, biological sex, physically/sexually attracted to, and emotionally/romantically attracted to. The goal should be to move beyond binaries and understand that gender and sexuality are fluid with various aspects that are too often misunderstood and lumped together as if they were the same. Much of the debates in mainstream media still reproduce the myth that there are only two genders (male and female) and that heterosexuality is the only "normal" sexual orientation.

The problematic nature of the male-female gender binary is shown in the story of Dutee Chand, a runner from India who in 2014 was disqualified from international competition due to her level of hormones. Gender verification tests have a history in sports for subjecting women (seldom men) to humiliating examinations and random rules about chromosomes, hormones, and physical features (Padawer, 2016). In response, Chand wrote a letter to the athletics federation of India: "I am unable to understand why I am asked to fix my body in a certain way simply for participation as a woman. I was born a woman, reared up as a woman, I identify as a woman and I believe I should be allowed to compete with other women, many of whom are either taller than me or come from more privileged backgrounds, things that most certainly give them an edge over me" (Padawer, 2016). After reviewing Chand's case, the Court of Arbitration for Sports temporarily suspended the International Olympic Committee's testosterone policy, but the debate over sex testing in sports continues.

Even the medical community is late to the table in the discourse on sexuality, finally removing homosexuality from the American Psychiatric Association's Diagnostic and Statistical Manual of Mental Disorders (DSM) in 1987 (Burton, 2015). Burton writes that the World Health Organization "only removed homosexuality from its ICD classification with the publication of ICD-10 in 1992." The role of science, religion, and media in reinforcing negative stereotypes about LGBTQ people and myths about gender has a long history and continues to reproduce heteronormativity and sexism (for reports about representation of gender in popular media see: Smith, Choueiti, Pieper, Case, & Choi, 2018; also, the Geena Davis Institute has a collection of reports at https://seejane.org/research-informs-empowers/). In order to challenge these misconceptions, students should explore the social construction of these ideas and the role media play today in reinforcing harmful stereotypes about gender and sexuality.

Recent studies of the predominance of male producers, directors, writers, and industry workers over women across a variety of fields have shown that the entertainment industry is still male-centric, and that women are subordinate throughout the spectrum of positions, jobs, and roles in the entertainment industry (Hunt, Ramón, Tran, Sargent, & Roychoudhury, 2018). In addition, during 2018, there has been an explosion of allegations of sexual abuse that the #MeToo movement has publicized and is fighting, sexual abuse from verbal harassment to rape across a variety of arenas. There have been powerful media exposés of abhorrent sexual abuse by former Fox News President Roger Ailes, CBS President Les Moonves, major film producers like Harvey Weinstein, actors like Bill Cosby, and a wide range of individuals in the talk show, entertainment, and news business.

As long as most of the people creating the messages are male, patriarchy is likely to continue. However, we have seen shifts in the media landscapes with more women becoming filmmakers, writers, directors, and actors. Many of these women struggle to create empowering roles for women and resist traditional stereotyped representations of women that limit narratives and images to presenting women as mothers, daughters, lovers, or individuals who are subordinate to men. Traditionally, Hollywood has privileged representations of women as mothers, romantic objects, or fallen "bad" women. "Good women" submitted to traditional roles and accepted subordination to men, whereas "bad women" defined themselves outside the boundaries of traditional women's roles and morality (Haskell, 1974). Hollywood film, radio broadcasting, and the early years of network television also enforced heteronormativity with entire genres, mainstream films, and TV series celebrating romantic relations between men and women, the family, and the norms of bourgeois morality, with those stepping outside of the norms often punished for "immorality." Furthermore, characters subtly coded as LGBTQ were often presented as outsiders, punished, or made fun of (Russo, 1995).

We should acknowledge, however, the shifting roles of men and women in media representations and the ways that representations of women have changed since the women's movements and sexual liberation movements of the 1960s. Previously, in Hollywood film, radio broadcasting, and early television in the 1950s, the dominant female genres such as melodrama and the women's film, women were represented as mothers or daughters in the family, romantic objects, or "bad women" who disrupted the bourgeois order (Haskell, 1974). Women also were represented in comedic roles in Hollywood comedies and television series like *I Love Lucy* and *Our Miss Brooks* where they were often the butt of jokes in ways that reproduced sexism. Today, however, film and television feature women in a variety of roles in government, industry, and positions of power, as well as a variety and diversity of personalities and sexualities.

In the last decade, the superhero genre in comics and movies have been challenging their previous stereotypes for race, gender, and sexuality by adding more diverse characters, such as a Black Captain America, a Muslim Pakistani American hero in Ms. Marvel, a transgender character as Batgirl #1, and a gay marriage between Kyle and Northstar. Curtis and Cardo (2018) attribute these changes to more women drawing and writing the comics and "partly due to the centrality of intersectionality and pluralism to third-wave feminism" (p. 282). In the past ten years, Marvel and DC comics each have added about a dozen new female characters (Curtis & Cardo, 2018).

Although representations of LGBTQ characters have improved, according to GLAAD's annual report on LGBTQ inclusion in television 2017–18, while these roles are increasing, they are still minimal with only 6.4% of regular characters identified as LGBTQ, as compared to 20% of Americans 18–34 who identify as LGBTQ (GLAAD Media Institute, 2018). Further, dominant forms of media culture engage in the objectification of women as Jean Kilbourne argues in her studies of advertising that show women being constructed largely as mothers, consumers, or sex objects. Indeed, media culture from the beginning, constructed women as objects of sexual desire, and women were encouraged by dominant forms of media culture to present themselves as alluring, sexy, well-dressed and made-up objects of desire. Furthermore, women were marginalized in media narratives which were characterized by men dominating women or exploring male subcultures in police, detective, military, doctor, lawyer or other genres that featured male culture and domination. To expose the marginalization of women, Alison Bechdel devised the Bechdel Test, which "is a method for evaluating the portrayal of women in fiction. It asks whether a work features at least two women who talk to each other about something other than a man" (https://en.wikipedia.org/wiki/Bechdel_test). Assigning students the Bechdel Test to interrogate gender representations in movies is an exercise that can illuminate the often problematic constructions of women in media.

Men, in turn, have been constructed in media representations as subjects who must seduce, conquer, and ultimately possess women to be appropriately male. Macho features of aggressiveness, toughness, and what Jackson Katz (2006) describes as "toxic masculinity," have been the norm for men across a variety of genres. Sports and the military are common domains in which toxic masculinity is constructed and acted out. Competitive professional sports teams are often organized on military models with the goal being to "destroy" the opposing team. Only relatively recently have studies shown the dangers to children and athletes from competitive body contact sports like football. Further, males are enculturated to be sports fans and the media have presented hours of sports events that socialize male and female viewers into values of competitiveness, individual success, and prevailing against other social groups. Indeed, since the rise of cable television in the 1990s, there have been entire sports networks where viewers can watch sports events 24 hours a day and 7 days a week.

On the other hand, sports can teach positive values like teamwork, fair play, cooperation, and submitting of the individual to the group. Sports has provided opportunities for people of color and working class people to obtain higher education, high-paying professional jobs, success, and other positive values. Sports has also been a domain enabling resistance as when star baseball players protested racism and segregation in the 1940s and 1950s, or Black athletes in the 1968 Olympics gave Black power salutes protesting continuing racism and the murder of African American leaders. And during the Trump administration, football players have taken a knee to the National Anthem to protest growing police violence against people of color, while other professional teams have refused invitations to the White House to protest the racist rhetoric and policies of Donald Trump.

The media, popular literature, and traditional male socialization have also constructed a toxic masculinity through identifying "being a man" with participating in gun culture. Many school shootings, and other mass shootings, have in common young male shooters who exhibit male rage and attempt to resolve a crisis of masculinities through violent behavior (Kellner, 2008). "Crises in masculinities" refer to a dominant societal connection between masculinity and being a tough guy, assuming what Katz (2006) describes as a "tough guise," a mask or façade of aggressive assertiveness, covering over vulnerabilities. The crises erupt in outbreaks of violence and societal murder, as super-angry men act out their rage, which can take extremely violent forms such as political assassinations, serial and mass murders, school, church, mosque, temple, and workplace shootings, as well as other forms of societal violence. Young men who engage in school shootings and gun violence exhibit a fetishism of guns or weapons, and engage in mass shootings orchestrated as media spectacle. The combination of male rage and crisis, mental health issues, media sensationalism, obsession with guns, and lax gun laws in countries like the United States is lethal and has led to the school shootings and mass gun violence that have plagued our era.

In addition, social media have also contributed to the dissemination of toxic masculinity through its speed, anonymity, social disembodiment, and the spread of new men's rights activists (MRAS) online communities known as the manosphere. Some of these groups refer to themselves as incels (involuntary celibates), betafags, geeks, and pick-up artists (PUAS). Debbie Ging (2017) suggests that growth of the manosphere has supported intense misogyny connected with online harassment, rape threats, death threats, and even the Oregon and Isla Vista mass shootings. Ging writes that the manosphere is a collection of communities linked to a philosophy derived from a scene in the movie *The Matrix* (1999) in which the character Neo decides to take the red pill. Ging explains, "The Red Pill philosophy purports to awaken men to feminism's misandry and brainwashing, and is the key concept that unites all of these communities" (p. 3). Donna Zuckerberg (2018) agrees that social media is exacerbating misogyny. She argues that many of the men promoting these misogynistic ideas on social media are appropriating ancient Greek and Roman philosophies, literature, and symbols that existed in a time when women had few rights. Zuckerberg states, these men are using "ancient literature to represent an aspirational ideal of a world they wish they inhabited. They idealise a model that erases much of the social progress that has been made in the last 2,000 years" (Iqbal, 2018). The manosphere is deeply misogynistic, disseminating violent rhetoric across the Internet and emboldening a movement of angry White men who view themselves as oppressed victims. This sense of male victimhood and violent masculine culture has led to violence against women through symbolic as well as physical actions.

Language can be a powerful tool to position audiences to read and think in certain ways. Often news reporting of male violence against women (commonly referred to indifferently as "domestic violence"), is presented in a passive voice, such as when CBS Miami headlined a story: "Miami-Dade Police Officer Arrested After Wife Ends Up In Hospital" (Tester, 2017). The use of the passive voice disassociates the subject who committed the crime from taking responsibility for his actions, as if the wife just landed in the hospital while coincidentally her husband was arrested. Lauredhel (2007) writes, "This ostensibly innocent bit of subject-camouflage has real consequences. If you can't see it, you can't fight it, and you can't blame it. The perpetrators of violence are rendered invisible. The culprits are shoved beyond the frame." In an active voice, "the man raped the woman." In a passive voice, "the woman was raped." And the ultimate transformation leaves the man completely out of the picture as language is used to label the victim as, "the raped woman." This use of passive voice can also be seen in reporting that is not favorable to the US, such as the case of the *New York Times'* initial headline describing the US bombing of a hospital in Afghanistan, "Airstrike Hits Hospital in Afghanistan, Killing at Least 9" (Norton, 2015). In an article for FAIR titled, "Media Can Tell Readers Who's Killing Whom – When They Want To," Naureckas (2018) provides examples of headlines from major news media in the passive and active voice. These can be excellent examples to share with students before having them search the Internet for their own examples.

Returning to our discussion of representations of women in US media culture, we should note that not all media culture is sexist, and that there have been exceptions to presenting women as subordinate to men. Hollywood has been famous for its top women stars such as Bette Davis, Joan Crawford, Jane Fonda, or Jennifer Lawrence playing strong women. Furthermore, occasionally toxic masculine behavior toward women has been portrayed as offensive and sexist. There have been representations of sensitive non-macho men in popular entertainment like some of the work of Marlon Brando, James Dean, Paul Newman, and contemporary male stars like George Clooney or Brad Pitt. Although hard masculinity was the traditional Hollywood ideal for men, the early decades of television presented some men as the knowing heads of families (*Father Knows Best*), professionals like doctors, lawyers, police, or soldiers, conditioning men to conform to dominant social roles and professions to reproduce and defend the existing society.

Likewise, since there are LGBTQ people in the entertainment industry, it is not surprising that there have been some positive portrayals of gay and lesbian relations even in the mainstream (see Russo, 1995). Although certainly there are fewer gay stereotypes in the media than before the rise of the gay liberation movements of the 1960s and 1970s, which protested such stereotypes, there are still all too many negative representations of homosexuality and narratives that villainize or make fun of LGBTQ people.

Yet, we must acknowledge that there have also been many changes in representations of gender and sexuality since the 1960s after the emergence of the women's liberation movements, sexual liberation movements, men's movements, and the revolution of values that took place in more progressive segments of US society concerning movements toward equality in gender, race, and class relationships. There have been and are movements organized against racism, sexism, homophobia, and other forms of prejudice in society and the media. These movements have called for stronger representations of women, people of color, and alternative sexualities in the media, while criticizing sexist, racist, homophobic and other objectionable representations.

Thus Hollywood film, network television, comic books, and other forms of media culture became a contested terrain from the 1960s through the present with many media texts presenting sexist, racist, homophobic and other objectionable representations, while some media producers and creators began to present stronger images of women, people of color, and alternative sexualities. In this context, it is important for students and citizens to question and protest media representations and narratives that produce and reproduce discrimination and oppression in all its myriad forms.

CHAPTER 3

Putting Theory into Practice

The theoretical base of critical media literacy provides a framework and road map for education to be critically empowering, developmentally appropriate and culturally responsive. There are many ways for educators to integrate critical media literacy in any subject area they teach. Elementary students can compare and contrast different versions of fables and fairytales, questioning portrayals of gender and race found in books, cartoons, movies, websites, songs, or video games. Then they can collaboratively create media with alternative perspectives or different endings of the same story, taking the form of comic strips, memes, podcasts, digital stories, or photographs. Older students can analyze movies to learn about production techniques, as well as question the way ideology is conveyed through characters, concepts, and places. Then they can create their own text, as advertisements, blogs, animation, zines, movie trailers, books, or social media, to retell or repurpose the story from different perspectives and challenge hegemonic narratives. The possibilities for creating various types of texts open the potential for students to be more creative, expressive, and critical than is likely when they are working just with print. These lessons involve many of the basic skills required in the CCSS from kindergarten on up, and by comparing different versions of the same story, students may begin to understand the constructed nature of information. Critical media literacy provides many benefits that include increasing: critical thinking, academic engagement, cultural relevance, and even empathy.

A middle school teacher in East Los Angeles found that after teaching a unit on critical media literacy to her eighth-grade students, not only did they develop better abilities to understand different points of view, but it also enhanced their level of empathy (Monarrez, 2017). Nikole Monarrez noticed a shift in the way her students were demonstrating their feelings about each other. She explains, "They were now taking into consideration how a situation might affect others before jumping to conclusions based solely on their own previous experience" (p. 45). This is an important concept now more than ever, as Sherry Turkle (2015) asserts that increasing use of social media seems to be causing decreasing levels of compassion. Turkle states that research has found "a 40 percent decline in the markers for empathy among college students, most of it within the past ten years. It is a trend that researchers link to the new presence of digital communication" (p. 21). Whether it is because of social media, or other factors, this decline in the ability to be empathetic is highly

© KONINKLIJKE BRILL NV, LEIDEN, 2019 | DOI: 10.1163/9789004404533_003

concerning and requires immediate attention. The focus of critical media literacy on issues of social and environmental justice directly links education with caring about others.

While it is more common for media education to be taught in the upper grades and in English courses, we now know that students of any age can and should engage with these ideas in all subject matters and as early as possible. Vivian Vasquez (2014) has demonstrated the potential for teaching preschoolers to think critically about their media and create podcasts, petitions, and songs. As young children learn to read visual images, watch and listen to stories, and interpret sounds, they can start applying critical media literacy skills to questioning the purpose, audience, and construction of all information and entertainment. They should be encouraged to ask critical questions in ways where the words are adapted to their level of understanding and cultural experiences. While we should not expect kindergartners to know high-level abstract concepts, we should expect them to wrestle with differences between right and wrong in the texts they are using. In a kindergarten classroom in South Los Angeles, five-year-old students learned to empathize with nature and then decided to create their own posters to educate other students at their school about taking care of the environment (Túchez-Ortega, 2017). Literacy is a powerful tool, and when students use it to communicate with real audiences for genuine purposes, the greater their power becomes to read and write the word and the world.

Teaching and Learning in an Image-Based Culture

Teaching students the skills to critically read visual images can be an excellent starting point for engaging young children, English language learners, and any students struggling with a print-dominant curriculum. Before children can speak, they are surrounded by visual images that become even more ubiquitous as they get older. This omnipresence of visual representations beckons educators to help students think visually about aesthetics, design, and the politics of representation.

Through using photography as a pedagogical tool, students can deepen their analysis skills and enhance their media-making abilities. There is a power that the photographic image conveys that no other medium can do in the same way. Photographs by Lewis Hines of children toiling in factories, contributed to the first child labor laws in the United States. In 2018, pictures of crying children being taken away from their parents by US immigration officers brought outrage from the public and politicians on both side of the aisle. Photographs have contributed to the starting and ending of wars, sending people to jail, inspiring political dissent, and even like Cupid's arrows, rousing people to fall in love. The photograph is said to be worth a thousand words because it transports us vicariously to experience a frozen moment in time; it permits us to see and feel the world beyond our touch and allows us to express our innermost feelings without speaking a single word.

> Photographs have a swifter and more succinct impact than words, an impact that is instantaneous, visceral, and intense. They share the power of images in general, which have always played havoc with the human mind and heart, and they have the added force of evident accuracy. (Goldberg, 1991, p. 7)

This assumption of accuracy combines with positivist notions about a single objective reality that leads many to consider photographs to be indisputable proof; they are permitted as evidence in a court of law and used by scientists to record data. Barthes (1981) states, "From a phenomenological viewpoint, in the Photograph, the power of authentication exceeds the power of representation" (p. 89). For people around the world, the photograph is a document that conveys truth and reality, while preserving history.

While photography can be an important instrument to record reality and document our present and past, it is also a device that can mislead and be misused. By as early as the 1850s, Louis Agassiz and other eugenicists were using photography to justify their theories about the racial inferiority of non-Europeans. Banta and Hinsley (1986) report that in the 1930s, similar racist ideas were promoted by Harvard University anthropologist Earnest A. Hooton, who claimed that his photographs of human skulls "furnished the ultimate proof of the validity of our morphological types" (p. 65). These days, the vast number of photographs in mainstream media that glamorize Whiteness and marginalize people of color continue the legacy of racial misrepresentation. The rampant use of Photoshop and digital manipulation on practically all advertising and magazine covers contributes to the popular ideals of beauty as Eurocentric, artificially skinny, and unattainable (Kilbourne, 2010).

Susan Sontag (1990) asserts, "Although there is a sense in which the camera does indeed capture reality, not just interpret it, photographs are as much an interpretation of the world as paintings and drawings are" (pp. 6–7). Photographs, no matter how realistic they look, are always a subjective representation, shaped by the photographer's choices of who and what to photograph, as well as the context of how, when, where and why to take the picture (Cappello & Hollingsworth, 2008; Share, 2003). The content that ends up inside the frame of any photograph is never neutral because it has been chosen and constructed by a subjective human being. While photography often seems to be objective and is given great storytelling authority, it is still just a human tool subject to all the limitations and frailties of any other medium of communication. It is this power of credibility that is given to photography that makes the camera an especially important tool to use and critique.

Everyone Today Is a Photographer

For many years, cameras have been primarily in the hands of professional photographers, visual artists, and photobuffs; yet now, with the popularity of tiny cameras embedded in computers, tablets, and cell phones, it seems that everyone is a photographer. New Web 2.0 applications and smaller faster hardware are making photography so common that millions of people are creating, sharing, and viewing photographs daily. Facebook, Instagram, Snapchat, Imgur, Flickr, and Pinterest are popular social media that capitalize on photography's powers and the technological ease of sharing images globally. According to a survey of adult internet users by the Pew Research Center's Internet Project, "Photos and videos have become an integral part of the online social experience...more than half of internet users post or share photos or videos online" (Duggan, 2013). One survey of youth in Massachusetts reports the percentages of students with cell phones as: 18–20% of third graders, 25–26% of fourth graders, 39% of fifth graders, and 83–84% of middle schoolers (Englander, 2011, p. 3).

Today's educators can benefit from digital cameras that cost less than a trip to the movies or cell phones with cameras that most students walk into the classroom with and are often forbidden to use. Once you have a digital camera, everything else is basically free; you can take as many pictures as you want. For educators, this makes photography an option for the classroom that even most financially strapped schools can afford. The costs are no longer prohibitive and the level of complexity has been simplified, making most cameras very user-friendly. However, since the technical skills for taking a picture are no longer required, that does not mean that people do not need to understand the visual literacy skills for critically reading and creating images. Part of the requirement for being literate in the 21st century is being able to read and write images, sounds, multimedia, and numerous other "multiliteracies" (New London Group, 1996).

It is the unique power of photography and the new ease of use, low cost and accessibility that has made the camera a practical tool for education to teach *with* and *about*. Wendy Ewald has been working for years with children and cameras, and argues for the potential of connecting art with education through photography. Ewald (2012) explains that "certain formal elements of photography such as framing, point of view, timing, the use of symbols, and observation of details...have parallels in writing" (p. 2). Since the 1960s, the folks at Foxfire have been taking cameras outside the classroom to document their Appalachian community and create their own publications, some of which became *New York Times* best sellers (Wigginton, 1991). These high school students have used cameras and tape recorders to challenge negative stereotypes of their families and friends as simple hillbillies, "people to be ignored." The students have taken pictures and written stories that documented the rich culture and assets they possess (Wigginton, 1972, p. 13).

Cameras in journalism or photography classes are not new, but cameras in elementary schools and secondary school science, math, history, and English classrooms are far more rare. As the technology changes and more students enter the classroom with cell phones that can record still and moving images, schools have new opportunities to integrate photography into instruction as never before (Cappello, 2011; Kolb, 2008; Schiller & Tillett, 2004). These new opportunities also require educators to embrace different ways of teaching, making learning more student-centered, project-based, collaborative, multimodal, and critical. Cappello and Hollingsworth (2008) state, "photography is best used where there is an understanding that reality is perceived or constructed" (p. 444). It is not enough to just teach with a camera, critical media literacy also requires teaching about the tool and medium of photography. When educators integrate media education with photography, much potential for learning can emerge, even with the very young. Schiller and Tillett (2004) report on their experience using cameras with kindergartners:

> Digital photography provided young children with the opportunity to present their views "about things that matter" in a medium taken seriously by adults and older children, as demonstrated by positive responses from older students at the school and the enthusiastic comments from the Kindergarten parents about the "professional" look of the children's photographs. (p. 413)

Digital cameras can transform students from passive recipients of information into active photographers and/or subjects of their own pictures, coconstructing knowledge and representing their ideas.

English Language Learners (ELLs) can create their own flash cards by photographing each other in action to learn adjectives (synonyms and antonyms), irregular verbs, and prepositions. These students can be challenged by the many aspects of English that they need to learn explicitly, aspects that native speakers acquire from hearing and using English repeatedly all around them (Krashen, 1992). Not continually surrounded by English, ELLs face considerable difficulty learning irregular verbs, nominalizations, prepositions, and the vast number of new adjectives and adverbs (Gibbons, 2009). It can be overwhelming to learn a second language while simultaneously trying to learn the content of different subject matter. Writing from over 30 years of experience teaching elementary school, Pat Barrett Dragan (2008) explains that for ELLs, photography:

> gives them a feeling of power and control over a piece of equipment, and that helps compensate for the lack of control they may feel over not yet speaking English. Photography gives my English language learners (ELLs) an additional language – another way for them to convey who they are and show what they know. (p. 41)

Susan Britsch (2010) reports that while there is little research available on using photography with young ELLs, it is important to recognize that "Language does not develop as an isolated mode of communication. Its relationship with visual imagery is primal" (p. 171). All students can use cameras to record their lives outside of school, as well as construct meanings of academic words and ideas they are learning in school.

In a fourth-grade classroom in downtown Los Angeles, students learned how to illustrate their vocabulary words with photography (Share, 2015a). First, they took pictures that showed words they encountered in their textbooks. The activity began with a class discussion about the meaning of the word and the different ways they could show it in a single image. The student photographer had to tell classmates where and how to pose in order for the picture to communicate the intended meaning of the word. They analyzed photographs from newspapers and magazines and brainstormed a list of techniques that photographers use to convey feelings and ideas, such as camera angles, composition, and lighting. After a couple weeks, students were so enthusiastic about taking pictures that they began bringing their own words into the classroom. This sparked an activity in which whoever brought in a new word would get to take the picture illustrating that word or be in the picture. Because of the enthusiasm, students spent 5–10 minutes every morning illustrating vocabulary words and generating a massive collection of new words. The digital images were imported into a PowerPoint file that became a synonym/antonym flash card game. Students wrote sentences or stories to accompany their photographs and then printed PowerPoint handouts that were folded into pocket-sized books for each student. Some of the PowerPoint handouts were printed on colored paper, laminated and cut up into popular trading cards. These personalized vocabulary cards and booklets were a huge hit with students and their families, as well as powerful student-made teaching materials to increase their vocabulary and literacy skills. This use of photography for learning different subject matter expands the understanding of literacy and opens the opportunity to critically analyze visual texts using the CML framework.

Jennifer Pineda (2014), a first-year teacher working in an inner-city classroom documented the benefits she encountered using photography to improve her first graders' writing. Before introducing photography to her class, her students were struggling with writing, finding it difficult and boring. When she told them that they would be taking pictures, Pineda states, "Cheers filled the room!" Pineda let her students use an iPad to take pictures of anything they wanted. She explains that the students did not need any help taking pictures and they loved the process. Their photographs became the motivation for their writing and each student wrote stories based on the photographs they took or brought in from home.

Pineda encouraged her students to work together to take pictures, discuss their photos, and then write about them. By orienting students to each other, the children were able to help each other take the pictures and talk through their writing. Pineda reports, "My students were gaining a clearer understanding of how to show a story with their writing versus simply telling." The best writing emerging from Pineda's students came from those who were writing about family photographs they brought from home. Pineda explains, "It was these students who were writing the most detailed stories. It seemed as though these students had strong connections with the pictures they were using because they had a vivid memory of the experiences they had in the moment the picture was taken." This was a powerful way to motivate the writing process and also validate students' *funds of knowledge* as they took pride in sharing about their lives beyond the classroom (González, Moll, & Amanti, 2005).

Taking pictures involves more than just making writing fun and motivating. Pineda states, "The process of using pictures that they took on their own made the story behind every picture important. They were truly engaged in their writing because every picture they took and used for their writing held a different experience in it." In other elementary classrooms in which teachers gave cameras to students to use as part of the writing process, Cappello and Hollingsworth (2008) found "the photographs were both process and product. Photographs and the photographic process provided the stimulus for writing, extended the meaning of the original texts (drafts), and encouraged complex thinking" (p. 448). These authors suggest that "[t]ransmediation, the process of interpreting meaning from one sign system to another is central to understanding the possibilities of photography in classrooms" (p. 444). When students move between various communication systems, be they oral language, print literacy or visual imagery, they discover connections and differences between the sign systems, something that enlarges and expands the meaning. The photographs did not replace print literacy – they enhanced the multiple literacy processes. Transmediation is an important aspect of CML because it helps students consider the medium and not just the message. When students analyze the various ways the same message can position an audience to think differently based on the medium of communication, they gain insight about the medium as well as the message. This moves teaching *with* media to teaching *about* media.

Photography is a wonderful medium to explore many concepts of visual literacy as well as a powerful pedagogical tool for the classroom. Students can use their cell phones or tablets to create photographs that illustrate vocabulary words for any subject matter. For Language Arts, students can take two photographs of each other; in one they try to make their peer look like the protagonist and in the other they represent the same student as the antagonist. This can help students think about character development while additionally learning visual literacy. Students can also use cameras to study their environment outside the classroom and consider the details and aesthetics for place-based writing and the relationships between humans and the natural world (Beach, Share, & Webb, 2017). This can also provide an insightful opportunity to reflect on the power involved with representing others and being represented by others. For students of color, this can be an opening to question and challenge the way mainstream media often portray people who look like them. For White students, critiquing media representations of "others" can be an entry point into *courageous conversations* about White supremacy, racism, and stereotypes (Singleton & Linton, 2006).

Aural Literacy

To help students understand the influence and potential of sounds, music, dialogue, and narration, they can analyze audio engineering by exploring the way sounds, words, and even sentences convey different meanings depending on the context in which they are created, voiced, and heard. There are codes and conventions for dialogue, narration, music, and sound effects that shape what and how the audience hears, thinks, and feels. For spoken language, inflection and tone influence the meanings of words, sometimes more than the literal definition. In a movie, words, sounds, and music are either diegetic (when the source of the sound is visible or assumed to be present) or non-diegetic, and that distinction contributes to how the audience makes sense of the show. These are important elements for students to analyze in audio texts, as well as valuable production skills students should learn for public speaking and creating their own audio recordings (Shamburg, 2009).

Students can learn about and experiment with *tone painting*, the way musical sounds conjure up ideas, feelings, and images. A few basic elements of music include:
– *Dynamics:* The loudness and softness (volume).
– *Timbre:* Every instrument has its own tone color.
– *Pitch:* The highness or lowness of notes in music.
– *Silence:* Time to think and for echoes to fade away.
– *Tempo:* The speed of the music, whether it is fast or slow.
– *Texture:* The amount of layers or voices (thick and thin).
– *Duration:* The length of each sound (long and short).
– *Rhythm:* Organization of sounds between the beats.
A common, yet invisible ingredient in most multimedia productions is the use of sound effects. Few video games, television shows, cartoons, or movies are created without a Foley artist adding sounds. When students create their own sound effects while reading books or telling stories, they creatively engage with texts on multiple levels that can access their intellectual, social, and emotional intelligences. Working together, students can create podcasts that allow their voices to be heard and provide counter-stories to challenge dominant narratives of race, class, gender, sexuality, or any topic they feel is being misrepresented or under-represented (Bell, 2010). Creating podcasts is easy and inexpensive; most cell phones have a voice memo feature that will digitize any sounds. Removing the visual elements can be a useful strategy to help students focus on just the aural modality and experience one medium of communication at a time. By having students take content from a visual or print-based medium and transmediate it into a podcast, they will learn about the strengths and limitations of different media. Much has been written about the first televised presidential debate; the 1960 Kennedy-Nixon debate in which audiences judged the candidates differently depending if they were watching on TV or listening on the radio (Botelho, 2016). Similarly, by having students create comparable messages in various media, students can analyze the role of the medium in the process of positioning the audience.

Multimodal Literacy

Since television, movies, and video games have accustomed youth to stories told with sounds and images, the combination of modalities for storytelling can make the process more significant. When combining aural and visual texts to create multimedia stories, it can be helpful to start by storyboarding ideas with simple sketches to accompany the written text. The storyboard is intended to support the writing process and help students plan the visual and aural elements along with the dialogue and narration. One of the considerations should include editing, planning how the images and sounds will blend, cut, transition, and interact. The pace and sequence of a movie influence how the images and sounds affect the audience.

There are numerous tools and strategies for making digital stories and they can be as simple as combining drawings with narration, or more sophisticated uses of movie-making programs that allow students to professionally edit their video. New applications available on cell phones support students to create stop motion animation, edit music and videos, and produce their own movies. It is necessary to find the appropriate tool for each situation, but the tool is just a means for the most important work of learning how to tell a story (Ohler, 2008). As the tools become more accessible and easier to use, students can create multimedia presentations on any subject matter to demonstrate their understanding and to challenge dominant myths and omissions.

The theory and pedagogy of critical media literacy can and should be applied at all grade levels and in all classes. The following are just a few examples: Math students can analyze how numbers are used to support or undermine issues with graphs and statistics, thereby demonstrating that all media, numbers, words, images, or sounds are social constructions (conceptual understanding #1: Social Constructivism). English teachers often have students explore persuasive writing, something that leads easily to analyzing and creating advertising. Learning about the power of words and language is something that applies to every medium of communication, often with different codes and conventions (conceptual understanding #2: Languages/Semiotics). Music instruction provides opportunities to explore the use of sounds in movies to tell stories and the ways songs of protest energize social movements. Through comparing various cultural contexts of music, students can gain perspective into the way audiences negotiate meanings depending on their experiences, beliefs, and culture (conceptual understanding #3: Audience/Positionality). History teachers play an important role in helping students understand different perspectives, multiple interpretations, and the power of who gets to tell the story (conceptual understanding #4: Politics of Representation). Physical education is a class that is ripe to unpack the inequality of gender representations in sports. Since male sports receive much more media coverage and economic support, students can investigate the economic motivations for the differences (conceptual understanding #5: Production/Institutions). Science students can analyze the way scientific concepts are represented and question who is most likely to benefit or be disadvantaged by the science. Historically, science has been used to support society's dominant stories, often influencing people to believe things they don't understand just because of the trust they endow to the "presumed objectivity" of science (conceptual understanding #6: Social and Environmental Justice).

Through deconstructing social media, news, movies, and advertising, students can question how science, math, history, and all languages are used to support ideas, frame issues, or sell products. It is important that students are not only reading, viewing, and listening to media, they should also be using and creating media. Therefore, students should practice producing genuine information as well as recognizing misleading data so that they become experts in detecting problematic representations, misleading information, and actual "fake news." As technologies continue to evolve, the potential for manipulation increases, such as "deep fake" videos that look like real people saying or doing things they had never done or said. The porn industry has used this technology to create fake movies of celebrities having sex and one deep fake video has already been used by a political party in Belgium. An example of this technology can be seen in a BuzzFeed video (https://tinyurl.com/ya8qev46) in which actor Jordan Peele voices the dialogue for images of Barack Obama appearing to insult President Trump (Schwartz, 2018).

Information communication technologies have opened new opportunities for progressive educators to revitalize education and empower youth to tell their own stories, question dominant ideologies, challenge oppressive systems and structures, and create alternative media that is more socially and environmentally just. Critical media literacy provides a framework to expand notions of literacy to be more inclusive of all types of texts and deepens the potential to question the power of the word, image, and sound bite to represent social and environmental injustice. When students learn to critically read and write with images, sounds, multimedia, and print, they deepen their critical thinking skills and develop their identities as responsible and empowered global citizens. The challenge to critically understand media texts, as well as the power to create and disseminate alternative messages, is the essence of critical media literacy.

The Dynamics of Digital and Networked Media

Twenty-first-century literacy skills require new understandings of literacy because people are participating in *multiliteracies* (New London Group, 1996), reading and writing photographs, music, movies, advertising, social media, popular culture, as well as printed books and magazines. With the popularity of cell phones and new mobile devices, youth are communicating and socializing daily in numerous ways, such as: blogging, instant messaging, photographing, pinning, tagging, texting, tweeting, podcasting, and videoing. The convergence of media corporations and new media platforms, along with technology's exponential growth are changing society and students to be more mediated and networked than ever (Jenkins, 2006; McChesney, 2015; Prensky, 2010).

For many teachers, digital writing may seem the same as writing with pencil and paper because it uses many of the same elements of print literacy and it is easy to turn a handwritten essay into a digital text; however, there are significant differences. Digital texts gain new potential to be *multimodal* (combining different formats), *hyperlinked* (connecting with other media and building new relationships), and *interactive* (allowing for sharing, remixing, and participation) (Beach, 2009). Digital reading and writing do not occur in isolation; they are embedded in mediated environments and networked publics that have unique qualities, especially in relation to notions of persistence, visibility, spreadability, and searchability (boyd, 2014). While digital and networked texts bring wonderful opportunities, they also come with their own limitations and new concerns since they are neither neutral nor transparent.

Digital texts, messages, posts, feeds, and communicative acts (Habermas, 1984) are becoming more central to the life of youth and those increasingly immersed in digital culture and social media than those communicated by non-networked media. The difference between networked and non-networked communication is an important distinction that educators and students need to consider because *audience, purpose, medium,* and *context* influence all communication. The larger audience garnered by these media can be useful for sharing information widely, connecting people, and networking groups on a local or global scale. However, networked media can create complications when messages are shaped for one particular audience, without an awareness of the networks of unintended audiences that can also access them. Social media are challenging old ideas of audience, media, and relationships between senders and receivers.

Along with these challenges, opportunities are arising for re-envisioning the potential of this media landscape. Carrington (2005) reports that the emergence of new media texts "situate contemporary children in global flows of consumption, identity, and information in ways unheard of in earlier generations" (p. 22). A half century ago, Raymond Williams (2009) wrote that the effects of television are less about discrete programs or messages and more about a *flow* of programming running day and night. According to O'Connor (2006), a critical point of Williams's analysis is the notion that the flow of television is constructed to prepare viewers for advertising. Today with the continual flow of information, entertainment, and social interactivity available on the Internet, Williams's notion of flow based on television viewing and advertising, has risen to an unprecedented level.

This evolving media landscape is blooming with opportunities for students to create and contribute to a new reality. Rather than evaluating information in search of a single "truth," students should be learning to search for different perspectives and evidence to triangulate findings and evaluate information from multiple sources. Oreskes and Conway (2010) assert that students need to be skeptical of everything, even science, which is often considered objective. "History shows us clearly that science does not provide certainty. It does not provide proof. It only provides the consensus of experts, based on the organized accumulation and scrutiny of evidence" (Oreskes & Conway, 2010, p. 268).

CML offers students a framework to hone their inquiry skills by guiding them to question the interconnections of power and information as they learn with and about media, technology, and popular culture. This is a lens and process for analyzing and creating meanings through which any content can be taught. Although CML is rooted in a rich history of cultural studies, CML pedagogy is not a content area to be siloed within the domain of one academic discipline. CML belongs in every classroom from preschool to university; it invites educators to teach with democratic pedagogy through an inquiry process that questions "common sense" assumptions.

Learning CML through Media Production and Praxis

Learning CML through production emboldens students to learn the codes of representation of their social world through producing media texts. Whether students create visual art or increase their computational literacy by developing their own video games, they empower themselves when they actively create new media. There is much pedagogical potential for students when they are involved in creating media that can push back and challenge dominant myths and stereotypes. As in print literacy, one learns to read by writing and to write by reading. Even though early media education recognized the value of student-produced media, US media education has "not necessarily advocated a critical stance toward media production" (Morrell, Dueñas, Garcia, & López, 2013, p. 4). It is with critical media pedagogy that Morrell et al. (2013) suggest educators need to enlighten "students about the potential they have, as media producers to shape the world they live in and to help to turn it into the world they imagine" (p. 3). Founder of the Educational Video Center in New York, Steven Goodman (2003) argues that one of the best strategies for "teaching critical literacy is for students to create their own media" (p. 6). Goodman (2010) explains that the process of creating documentaries holds many promising practices, such as:

> ensuring that all students contribute to discussions and decision making; use the community as a source of knowledge and information; connect personal experiences to social concerns; use multiple modes of literacy in their daily work; develop critical questions to guide their inquiry; revise their work and reflect on their learning; and use their video to inspire community dialogue and action. (p. 52)

The process of creating media has numerous pedagogical benefits. First, actively creating media, as opposed to merely reading and discussing it, is better constructivist pedagogy. Students learn best by doing and engaging their creative potential to construct meaning while also analyzing and critically reflecting on the messages they read and create (Dewey, 1963; Piaget, 1974; Vygotsky, 1978). In a student-centered approach to technology integration, Ching, Wang, Shih, and Kedem (2006) had kindergartners and first grade students take turns using a digital camera in their classroom to photograph anything they wanted. The researchers noted that while technology in classrooms is mostly used by teachers, when the students are given a camera, it can change the classroom dynamics and increase student access and empowerment. Ching et al. (2006) report that when students became photographers, "they had more leeway to deviate from their normal activities to roam around the learning environment and document various aspects of it" (p. 359). They explain:

> The students were able to appropriate digital photography and use it as a means to shift from their usual roles as restricted participants in worlds where others make the rules (Carere, 1987), and engage in sophisticated negotiations with their fellow students as photographic subjects and within the norms of classroom behavior. (p. 366)

Second, creating alternative media is empowering because it provides students a path for taking action about the problems they see and encounter in the world around them. Students need to know how to use new tools to engage politically in their world in ways that can reach countless numbers of people, much as they do socially on their own with gaming, texting, Snapchat, Instagram, Twitter, etc. Web 2.0 is about sharing and social media provide the platforms and the potential to do just that (Prensky, 2010). According to the editors at Rethinking Schools:

> If we ask the children to critique the world but then fail to encourage them to act, our classrooms can degenerate into factories of cynicism. While it's not a teacher's role to direct students to particular organizations, it is a teacher's role to suggest that ideas need to be acted upon and to offer students opportunities to do just that. (Bigelow, Christensen, Karp, Miner, & Peterson, 1994, p. 5)

Prensky (2010) asserts that real learning "involves students immediately using what they learn to do something and/or change something in the world. It is crucial that students be made aware that using what they learn to effect positive change in the world, large or small, is one of their important roles in school" (p. 20). He explains that digital technology provides useful tools to do this:

> Even elementary school students can change the world through online writing, supporting and publicizing online causes, making informational and public service videos and machinima, and creating original campaigns of their own design. Anything students create that 'goes viral' on the Web reaches millions of people, and students should be continually striving to make this happen, with output that both does good and supports their learning. (Prensky, 2010, p. 66)

This type of social justice education using real-world digital projects is vital because the world is not "flat" (with a level playing field) as Thomas Friedman (2005) claims; there are still tremendous problems of inequality and injustice. However, new technologies are reshaping our environment and social relations, providing more opportunities for students to create media that can challenge problems, promote social justice, and enhance academics.

CML pedagogy encourages students to identify injustice, to analyze its roots and the ways in which it propagates, and to take action to challenge the problem. Students can learn, by engaging with the six CML questions and concepts, about any media message; however, by engaging with media as producers, students not only learn essential digital literacies, they also gain a sense of agency and empowerment to foster social justice. Like any good project-based learning, the *process* of creating a product is usually where most learning occurs. Teachers should be cautious not to fall into the common trap of over-valuing the final product at the expense of the creation process. CML emphasizes the application of critical thinking inquiry skills as well as media production that can be used to address genuine concerns.

Storytelling

Long before the invention of the printing press, storytelling was a multisensory experience, place-based and rich in expression, interaction, and relationships. Many of these old qualities of personal interactions are possible with new media that incorporate sounds, visuals, and movement. Teachers can have students interview their elders and community members about the local history to learn about the past from primary sources, the people who lived it. These interviews can be combined with images and music to create multimedia presentations, documentaries, or a community archive. The possibilities for creating various types of texts open the potential for students to be more creative, expressive, and critical than is likely when they are just writing an assignment for class.

Indigenous pedagogy provides examples of the power of oral storytelling, the use of metaphor and analogy to convey ideas beyond the literal meanings of words, the social value of interviewing elders and people whose voices are often marginalized or ignored, and the importance of nature-based knowledge (Arrows, 2013). For tens of thousands of years, people around the world have been passing along their values and entire cultural identities through oral traditions. About 500 years ago, following the invention of the printing press, in many parts of the world, print literacy flourished as oral storytelling waned. "Thus, the richness of oral communication was lost, which includes, from all points of view, a significant dimension of musicality, proxemics, gestural communication, spatial relationship, specific closeness and sensorial perception between those speaking" explain Tornero and Varis (2010, p. 106). Fortunately, many indigenous societies have continued to practice and preserve the tradition of oral storytelling, a distinctly human social practice that remains a powerful space for teaching and learning. Many aspects of indigenous pedagogy can benefit educators and students, such as oral storytelling that aligns better with visual and aural modalities of audiovisual media than it does with print-based literacy. Four Arrows (2013) writes:

Although the Indigenous approaches may seem strange at first to some teachers, they will likely resonate at some level. All of us have ancestors who once lived in one place long enough to understand how to exist in relative harmony with the rhythms of the natural world. This nature-based knowledge is in our DNA. (p. 2)

CHAPTER 4

Preparing Educators to Teach Critical Media Literacy

Even though youth are immersed in a world in which media and technology have entered all aspects of their lives and society, few teacher education programs are preparing teachers to help their students to critically understand the potential and limitations of these changes. It is crucial that new teachers learn *how* to teach their K-12 students to critically read and write everything, from academic texts to social media.

This means that schools of education responsible for training the new wave of teachers, must be up-to-date, not just with the latest technology, but more importantly, with critical media literacy theory and pedagogy. This preparation is essential to help teachers and students think and act critically, with and about, information communication technology (ICT), media, and popular culture. Unfortunately, there are few teacher education programs anywhere in the world that are teaching this (Hobbs, 2007). In Canada, where media literacy is mandatory in every grade from 1–12, most new teachers are not receiving media literacy training in their pre-service programs (Wilson & Duncan, 2009). Researchers investigating media education in the United Kingdom (the place where many of the ideas about media literacy first emerged) found that many teachers are unprepared to teach media education and "[t]here is only limited training available to prepare schoolteachers for teaching about the media" (Kirwan, Learmonth, Sayer, & Williams, 2003, p. 51).

While it is difficult to know for sure who is and who is not teaching critically about media and technology (Mihailidis, 2008), there seems to be an increase in media literacy courses in higher education in the United States (Stuhlman & Silverblatt, 2007). As technology and media continue to evolve and move into more public and private spaces, more educators are recognizing the need for training new teachers about media literacy (Domine, 2011; Goetze, Brown, & Schwarz, 2005; Hobbs, 2007) and some are even addressing the need to teach about critical media literacy (Flores-Koulish, Deal, Losinger, McCarthy, & Rosebrugh, 2011; Luke, 2000; Robertson & Hughes, 2011). Through analyzing 316 US public educational institutions that provide teacher training and graduate studies, researchers Tiede, Grafe, and Hobbs (2015) found that very few offer more than media didactics (basic educational technology that teaches *with* media, not *about* media). They report, "Media education, with emphasis on the instructional practices associated with the critical evaluation of media, culture, and society, were scarce, representing only 2% of all study programs in teacher training programs" (pp. 540–541).

In 2011, the United Nations Educational, Scientific, and Cultural Organization (UNESCO) published a curriculum guide online in ten different languages for training teachers in media education (Grizzle & Wilson, 2011), "thereby underlining that teacher training in media and information literacy will be a major challenge for the global education system at least for the next decade" (Pérez-Tornero & Tayie, 2012, p. 11). UNESCO takes an approach to media education that combines media and information literacy (MIL). Carolyn Wilson (2012) explains that MIL includes many competencies, from learning about and using information communication technologies to:

> the ethical use of media, information and technology, as well as participation in democratic and intercultural dialogue. MIL is both a content area and way of teaching and learning; it is not only about the acquisition of technical skills, but the development of a critical framework and approaches. (p. 16)

Teaching Teachers CML

Transforming education to critically use media, technology, and popular culture for social and environmental justice is the overarching goal of a critical media literacy course at UCLA's teacher education program. Through combining theory from cultural studies and critical pedagogy with practical classroom applications of new digital media and technology, this course attempts to prepare K-12 educators to teach their students how to critically analyze and create all types of media.

In the CML course, full-time teachers working on their master's degree and pre-service teachers earning their teaching credential and master's degree use cameras, computers, cell phones, and tablets to explore their communities in search of connections with math, science, and social studies, to reflect on their personal identities, to express their feelings and thoughts, to tell stories, to collaborate, and to challenge dominant ideologies. Through various lessons, students demonstrate their competence with digital media and their understanding of the politics of representation. The course involves lectures and assignments structured to integrate technology, popular culture, and media analysis, as well as production so that students not only critically analyze and become better readers, but also learn to create with these new tools and become 21st-century writers. This expanded notion of literacy tends to resonate with many who have grown up playing and socializing regularly with media and technology, as they find it more culturally relevant than just print-based literacy.

The challenge is to combine this expansive view of literacy with a deeper exploration of the ever-present connections between information and power. The more critically empowering aspect of the class is the engagement with ideology, power, and identity in the literacy process. This critical analysis and use of literacy as a tool for civic participation, emphasizes the essential role that literacy can play in social justice education.

The first class introduces the CML framework with its six conceptual understandings and questions, and then each session that follows starts by reviewing and applying those concepts and questions. Since one goal of the course is for new teachers to understand that literacy includes reading and writing all types of texts, we encourage students to analyze as well as produce media. A series of assignments require students to work together to create various types of media projects such as wanted posters, photographs, podcasts, memes, digital stories, social media, etc. The students are also expected to work collaboratively on a CML lesson plan/learning segment that they write-up, present to the whole class, and when possible, also teach in their student teaching placement.

One of the initial activities students engage in is to create a visual poster about somebody in the class whom they do not know well. For this assignment, students visually represent a peer without showing the person's face or name. They interview their colleague for just five minutes in class and then for homework they create a poster about her/him using only visual imagery: photographs (of anything but the person's face), drawings, logos, etc. The following week, they display their posters for everyone to see in a gallery walk. During the debrief, students discuss what it feels like to be represented visually, as well as how it felt to represent somebody else using only images. For some, this is challenging, as they visually generalize qualities of their peer while trying to avoid stereotypes. This leads to conversation about critical media literacy conceptual understanding #4 (Politics of Representation) and the ways images in media often stereotype groups of people.

The following assignment requires students to produce a more involved poster using images, words, and various elements of design. Students are tasked with creating a *wanted poster* that visually represents something they are teaching. This is intended to integrate media into the curriculum in order to make subject matter more engaging while also teaching computer literacy, visual literacy, and critical media literacy. This assignment is an opportunity to see how to take any lesson they are teaching and combine media and technology with images and sparse text to create a media product that authentically demonstrates content matter understanding. As teachers create their wanted posters, they see that anything can be the subject matter (math formulas, scientific concepts, books, letters, numbers, historical events, and even people).

The task also serves as an introduction to basic technology skills such as inserting an image into a Word document, using Word Art for a title, including a border, and adding text boxes – a *description* and a *warning*. The assignment requires teachers and students to think about visual literacy and consider typography (type of font, color, size), photography, illustration, composition, and design (conceptual understanding #2: Languages/Semiotics). In order for students to *transmediate* the information they are learning into visual language, they need to synthesize the ideas into a single image, title, and brief text that will describe it and warn the reader about it.

The wanted posters that the new teachers create become original examples for their own students to see digital alternatives for demonstrating learning and the potential for reframing discourse about whose story is seen and heard in the classroom. While the wanted poster can simply be a way of retelling information, it can also become a more critical media literacy tool for creating media about ideas, people, and events that have been misrepresented or under-represented in textbooks and popular culture. Verma Zapanta, a social studies student teacher, created a wanted poster of Gabriela Silang, an indigenous woman in the Philippines who led her people in armed resistance against colonial domination. When teachers and students have the opportunity to produce their own representations, they can appropriate the power to determine whose stories are told and how. The wanted poster is one of the most common assignments from the course that is taken directly into the classroom where elementary and secondary students create their own posters. It is an activity that can be done with computers to integrate technology skills with subject matter learning, as well as with just paper and markers in schools with limited access to technology.

Exploring Identity and Media Representations

As teachers and students recognize the power of visual representations, we problematize the process of representation to reflect on negative media portrayals they find of themselves. Students use Voicethread.com, an online social media site, to create their *Through Others' Eyes* assignment that involves posting and commenting about an aspect of their identity that they have seen maligned in the media. Voicethread provides the opportunity for students to see and hear each other's reflections, and to add comments to their peers' postings. In addition to providing experience with more sophisticated technology than the simple manipulation of images and text in the wanted poster, this assignment requires students to critically analyze media representations and push back at negative messages that saturate their world. In doing so, students have critiqued the portrayal of body image, immigration, domestic violence, alcoholism, religion, stereotypes, and the intersections of racism, sexism, classism, and homophobia. These critiques help students explore the influence of visual images and the deep connection that media can have with power and identity, especially when representations are negative (conceptual understanding #6: Social & Environmental Justice). Amaris Leiataua (2013), a secondary social studies pre-service teacher, describes the impact of this assignment for her:

> Of all the projects we had to complete, the Voicethread assignment was the most powerful for me. This assignment gave me the opportunity to reflect on how my identity as a Pacific Islander womyn is negatively portrayed in the media. Even though I had already known my colleagues for a quarter, I was still hesitant to share something this vulnerable with them. After spending lots of time writing up a script and recording the voice over at least a dozen times before publishing it, I finally shared it. In response to my Voicethread, many people told me that they loved it and respected it or could resonate with what I expressed. This was an amazing experience to be able to connect with other peers who I thought I would never have anything in common with. They were very supportive. The stories that other people told also increased my awareness of their identity and made me respect them even more.

This assignment has often opened dialogue for addressing microaggressions (Sue, 2010) that too often go unseen by those who are not the targets. One example was created about the Mexican LEGO toy that generalizes all Mexicans as wearing a large hat, serape, and holding maracas, something one Latino student used to explain that when he hears the comment, "you look Mexican," it always carries a negative connotation. It is common during class, and in the online forum discussions for students to voice their surprise about the different Voicethread postings as concepts/ideas they had never thought about before. These discussions often become *courageous conversations* (Singleton & Linton, 2006) that need to be facilitated with respect and support. One of the biggest challenges for some students is to recognize the roles that power, privilege, and ideology play in determining the difference between individual acts of discrimination and social systems of oppression. Johnson (2006) explains that individualistic thinking "makes us blind to the very existence of privilege, because privilege, by definition, has nothing to do with individuals, only with the social categories we wind up in" (p. 77).

After experiencing their own issues of misrepresentation, students explore theoretical foundations of ideology and cultural studies. We begin with a heterosexual questionnaire for students to answer independently and reflect on their own ideas about sexuality from a perspective that challenges heterosexuality as the norm. In order to fill-out the survey, we request students pretend they are heterosexual, regardless of their sexual orientation. The survey is a pedagogical tool that is not collected or shared; it is only used to encourage students to think about the questions and their implications. A couple of questions are: "What do you think caused your heterosexuality? Is it possible your heterosexuality is just a phase you may grow out of?" (Rochlin, 1995). While some students laugh and some express discomfort, this questionnaire is intended to challenge dominant heteronormative ideas that are too often represented as "normal" in commercial media. The goal of this session is to disrupt hegemonic ideologies and expose them as social constructions, something that is often difficult for people who have not considered their social categories as privileges. By discussing the *Through Others' Eyes* postings, students see numerous examples of the ways that media privilege some at the expense of others. We connect the discussion with readings and further examples about ideology that highlight the notions of *naturalizing* and *othering* (Hall, 2003).

Numerous examples are provided to deconstruct "commonsense" assumptions of languages, labels, and even maps. One of the more powerful examples we view is a video clip from *The Colbert Report* (Colbert, 2009) on Comedy Central in which Stephen Colbert uses humor to explain the "Neutral Man's Burden." This is a clever use of satire to demonstrate how the appointment of Sonia Sotomayor, the first Latina nominated to the US Supreme Court will "destroy the neutrality of the Court" that has for years been predominantly White, male, and as Colbert reports, "neutral." We follow up this viewing with a metaphor of riding a bicycle in the wind to demonstrate how when the wind is helping you, most people don't notice it (like when you benefit from dominant ideologies). However, when the wind is blowing in your face and making riding the bicycle more difficult, most people feel the wind and recognize the problems it is creating (like the ability to recognize structures of oppression when you are negatively impacted by them). We encourage students to question the way dominant ideologies function to favor certain beliefs over others, which more often than not are ideas that benefit the groups having the most privilege. Marx and Engels wrote in 1846, "in every epoch, the ruling ideas are the ideas of the ruling class" (1970, p. 64). Understanding the way ideologies are reproduced in media helps students connect conceptual understanding #1 (Social Constructivism) with #4 (Politics of Representation) to interrogate issues of racism, classism, sexism, heteronormativity, and environmental justice, since all media messages are constructed within hierarchies of power.

Freire and Macedo (1987) remind us that "reading the world always precedes reading the word, and reading the word implies continually reading the world" (p. 35). Many of the activities and lectures in this CML course situate youth engagement, dialogue, and pedagogical reflection within the lived experiences that each student brings to the classroom. A focal point for the lessons is deliberative reflection on how ideologies stem from the cultural readings of our virtual, mediated, and physically experienced world. In her final reflection for Ed466, secondary school math teacher Monica Padilla (2013) states:

> As a Latina who attended urban public schools I am still struggling with insecurities that are a direct result of growing up in a marginalized community. Thanks to this program and this class I know that I can and must change that for my students. I want to empower my students to become active, critical participants in the creation of their own knowledge.

Engaging Race and Gender

Feminist standpoint theory offers an important theoretical lens for critical media literacy because it explains how beginning inquiry from a subordinate position can increase the likelihood of seeing the dominant ideology (Harding, 2004). As we explore the politics of representation, we address issues of race and racism in media using the four lenses of Afro-Media Literacy: slavery, eugenics, economics, and colorism (Byard, 2012). A powerful documentary that provides historical context about the social construction of race and racism is the BBC's *Scientific Racism: The Eugenics of Social Darwinism* by David Olusoga (Daniels, 2013). Using the Afro-Media Literacy framework reveals the historical connections among imperialism, colonialism, science, slavery, and colorism with current portrayals of African Americans in news media and popular culture.

While we study the ways in which many groups of people suffer from racist ideologies, we also focus specifically on African American and Native American experiences, since they continue to be groups heavily impacted by overt racism, disproportionate rates of incarceration and violence, deficit thinking, and racial microaggressions. One revealing activity we do in class involves going online to eBay.com and searching "collectable Americana." Every time students have visited this website, they have found people buying and selling racist images and items of African Americans, such as vintage porcelain figurines of Black Mammys and Sambos.

In order to analyze current expressions of colorism, students compare magazine covers of famous people of color that offer distinctly different examples of skin pigmentation. They also explore the white bias of popular cell phone apps that apply filters for photographs. This is the representational equivalent of whitening creams, hair straighteners, and cosmetic surgery. Mulaudzi (2017) describes the filters:

> When applied, a user's face morphs into a brighter, often light-skinned, blemish-free and slimmed down version of the original, sparkly-eyed and with a small nose. You may even end up with thinner, different coloured lips and blushed cheeks. Put simply, facial features are tweaked to suit Western standards of beauty.

These filters are so popular that many students have used them without considering the role of filters in perpetuating colorism.

We also discuss Orientalism, anti-Semitism, racism against Latinos and Asians, the model minority myth, and the intersections of all these stereotypes with gender, class, sexual orientation, and numerous other identity markers. This exploration of the social construction of race and racism demonstrates how the repetition of racist ideology contributes to racial microaggressions that are now less overt, but still highly damaging.

The media production assignment for this session requires students to work collaboratively to create a *racial myth-busting meme*. Students search cyberspace for a media image they feel is racist and then repurpose it into a meme that challenges the racism of its message. Even though there are numerous free meme creators online and plenty of search engines that can help students find racist images, this assignment is not easy, as it requires high-level thinking skills and creativity to produce a meme that in just a few words can challenge racism. Again, it is the process and not the product that produces the best learning. In this case, many of the final products that students struggled with the most generated the best discussions and the most lessons learned.

After taking the Ed466 course, a new science teacher turned his ninth-grade biology class into a CML inquiry. As his students were studying DNA and genetics, Alexander Dinh posed the question to his students, "Where do racial categorizations come from?" To answer this question, his students split into inquiry teams to research and then create Public Service Announcement (PSA) videos to explain their findings. Using their cell phones to film and edit, students unpacked the science about transcription and DNA translation as well as discussed the ways science has been misused to promote racism. In one PSA, the students report:

> The idea of genetics causing racism has constantly been twisted and turned in all sorts of directions. Ninety-nine percent of our genes are similar to all around us. That one percent is what makes us unique and apart from everyone else. Yet, society creates racism. Looks and appearances, judging of one another, [telling] racial jokes, are what racism is and it needs to be stopped. All must be informed about what genetics are to fully understand the concept of racism. (Stop Racism, 2013)

This project highlights the transdisciplinary nature, and potential, of CML pedagogy. While conducting their research, the students learned not only about biology, but also about how biology as a field can be used to uphold a dominant ideology. Moreover, the students learned how to construct a convincing narrative using what they learned in science to open the minds of people viewing their PSA online, as well as their peers in the course and at their high school.

It is important for students to understand that literacy is a process that requires analysis as well as production, reading and writing. In order to be media literate, students must learn to critically read messages as well as create them. It is often through the process of making media that students deepen their critical understandings and develop a sense of empowerment by producing counter-narratives or telling stories rarely heard. Student teacher Lizzette Mendoza (2016) writes in her final reflection:

> In this class, I thought deeply about how I am represented in the media, as a woman of color. These were ideas I have always thought of in passing, but did not delve into very deeply very often because they bother me a lot and many times I am not sure what to do with that anger and frustration. I saw that I can challenge those images by creating my own media and sharing it with students and peers.

In the following session, we move our focus from race to gender to compare and contrast representations of women and men in commercial media. Using constructivist pedagogy, we start with student input by having the class create two large collages on the classroom wall. Students rip out and tape on the wall pictures from popular magazines that they feel are typical of how women and men are most often represented in commercial media. Once the collages are complete, students discuss what they notice about the similarities and differences between the representations of men and women. This discussion attempts to analyze limitations of the male/female binary and is followed up with video excerpts from Jean Kilbourne's *Killing Us Softly 4* on images of women in advertising and Jackson Katz's *Tough Guise 2* on media representations of violent masculinity. The different perspectives and the media examples they provide add depth to the classroom discussion. We also go online and use an interactive tool for seeing and hearing different ways gender is constructed to sell toys to children. The Gender Advertising Remixer app (http://www.genderremixer.com) allows anyone to remix toy commercials by overlaying the sound track from commercials targeting girls with visual images of commercials targeting boys, or vice versa. This app was created by Jonathan McIntosh in 2010 and he has continued to update it with the help of others and fair use. The Gender Advertising Remixer and the gender collages work well with university graduate students and K-12 public school students to demonstrate how media construct gender roles.

Challenging Advertising and Consumerism

Since commercial media are for-profit businesses and advertising is their motor, we spend an entire class looking at advertising, marketing, and public relations. This session directly addresses conceptual understanding #5 (Production/Institutions) as we discuss media ownership, corporate mergers, government deregulation, merchandising, branding, and the latest marketing strategies for reaching eyeballs and collecting consumer data. Students analyze consumerism as a dominant ideology and read about how the rise of public relations has affected the decline of journalism (Sullivan, 2011). A consumerist society is an unsustainable model for a finite planet and with the increasing impact of climate change, we embrace the need for educators to address environmental justice with their students. In an attempt to meet this need, we are developing critical media literacy lessons that question humans' relationships with nature and the role of media in shaping these relationships in the past, present, and future (see Chapter 5).

To dissect an example of advertising that most students are likely to see, we pass out a palm-sized liquid yogurt smoothie to each student and have them answer the six critical media literacy questions about the product they are holding. After they have shared their ideas, they peel off the shrink-wrap packaging/advertising and expose the sterile white plastic bottle. Students reassess the product they hold in their hands based on this generic-looking bottle that no longer contains the colorful illustrations that previously made it seem more interesting.

With identical white plastic containers, students work in teams to transform their bottle back into a sellable product for various target audiences. Teams are given a list of different demographic groups from which to choose in order to create an advertisement to sell the same white bottle to their target audience. Students use markers and large sheets of chart paper to design their ad with any elements they want to use, from logos and mascots to full-blown jingles and role-playing. The activity provides an opportunity for students to rethink product packaging and create niche advertising that uses the codes and conventions of marketing and popular culture (conceptual understanding #2: Languages/Semiotics). It also encourages students to reflect on the ways people are target marketed, based on assumptions about their age, race, gender, class, and other identities (conceptual understanding #3: Audience/Positionality).

Creating Critical Media Literacy Lessons

About halfway through the quarter, student teams begin sharing their own critical media literacy lessons with the class. Every week from this point on, different groups of students present an abbreviated demonstration of the lesson or unit that they have designed to teach to their students. These lessons integrate the academic content they are required to teach with critical media literacy concepts and pedagogy. After each lesson is presented, the students in the audience provide feedback and ask questions. These lesson plan presentations have become a favorite part of the class for students and instructors, as many teams have developed creative new lessons for teaching critical media literacy in various subject areas, from primary language arts and social studies to secondary math and science. Examples of lessons that have been shown in class include the following:

- Elementary school teachers developed a Language Arts lesson comparing and contrasting different versions of fables and fairy tales with a Venn diagram. Students then work collaboratively to create comic strips with alternative perspectives of the same story. Along the same line, another team had students create movie trailers advertising a book from different perspectives, other than the narrator's or main characters' point of view.
- Elementary social studies teachers created a lesson for students to research California Missions (4th grade) or national landmarks (5th grade) and then create fictitious webpages, with templates to look like Yelp or TripAdvisor,

providing information about the location with multiple perspectives explaining the history of what happened to different groups (Native Americans, colonists, immigrants, African Americans), posting their comments as if they were reviewing the location. Some groups have had their students use templates that look like Facebook or even cell phone screens to retell and repurpose texts.

- Secondary science teachers created a series of lessons to help students distinguish between science fact and fiction in popular culture. Students explore how TV shows and movies often stretch the truth about science by focusing on one particular scientific inaccuracy; then they create a visual representation (movie poster, blog review, comic strip, etc.) of their analysis and reasoning about the scientific fallacy.
- Secondary math teachers designed a unit of lessons for students to analyze how graphs and infographics can distort information by challenging the way news media and advertising present data visually. Some examples of graphs they shared include bar graphs on housing prices zoomed in on maximum home values instead of including all housing costs, line graphs with an altered y-axis scale to distort the visual relationship between x and y values, and two-dimensional versus three-dimensional graphs that change the viewing angle and size of actual data. After analyzing the examples, students work in teams to create their own distorted graphs intended to skew information and mislead their audience.

Social Media and Partnering Pedagogy

In the critical media literacy class, student teachers explore social media and online applications for creating word clouds, thinking maps, cartoons, animations, gifs, memes, infographics, maps, digital stories, presentations, tutorials, rubrics, and more. Students share their knowledge about online resources; since apps change so often, there are usually students who can demonstrate new tools they have discovered. We also discuss the process of searching and tagging information; two sides of the same coin. The better students become at categorizing and labeling their data, the more skilled they will be at finding the information they want, since the same process involved in selecting file names and tags is necessary for choosing keywords for searching. We engage with Sofiya Umoja Noble's (2013) work critically examining the biases of search engines to help students understand that even the medium through which information passes influences the messages and the audience. We explore hoax websites as a way to challenge students' abilities to evaluate information. The Hoax Museum blog has a large collection (http://www.museumofhoaxes.com/), providing numerous examples to encourage students to triangulate their evidence and evaluate information from multiple sources.

In order to meet the requirements for a state teaching credential, we also focus on the California Commission on Teacher Credentialing (CCTC) compliance issues, including computer literacy, copyright, online safety, netiquette, and acceptable/responsible use policies. Accompanying these issues, we discuss fair use, remixing, open source, net neutrality, creative commons and the copyleft movement (Ferguson, n.d.; Hobbs, 2010; Ludwig, 2014; National Council of Teachers of English [NCTE], 2008). There is considerable misinformation among educators about the restrictions of copyright, and this tends to lead teachers to veer away from using media and popular culture in the classroom. It is important that teachers and students understand how *fair use* provides significant latitude to use copyrighted material in the classroom and in their media production, especially when the use is *transformative*. Fair use helps teachers see the connections between their legal rights and their classroom teaching. It is also essential for educators to understand the changing rules and regulations that are being fought in the courts regarding net neutrality and open access to the Internet.

Most students bring a mixture of prior knowledge, skills, and attitudes about technology, media, and especially video games. In an attempt to encourage an atmosphere of non-judgmental critique, we examine James Gee's (2007) ideas about lessons that educators can learn from video games, such as the need to take risks, lower the consequences of failure and provide immediate and non-judgmental feedback. Even long-time gamers are often caught off guard by Gee's positive perspective on the lessons we can learn from gaming.

Prensky (2010) suggests that "the key change and challenge for all 21st century teachers is to become comfortable not with the details of new technology, but rather with a different and better kind of pedagogy: partnering" (p. 3). Prensky (2010) calls for inquiry-based learning and a change in the conventional roles that students and teachers have played; now the teacher should be less of the expert calling the shots and more the facilitator, guide, or coach while students become active researchers and "world changers" (p. 20). This partnering pedagogy follows the traditions of Socrates' dialectical approach of thoughtful questioning, John Dewey's ideas of hands-on experiential learning, and Paulo Freire's call to replace banking education with problem-posing pedagogy.

This type of social justice education with real-world digital projects is vital because there are tremendous problems in the world and students need to learn that they can be part of the solution. New technologies are reshaping our environment and social relations, providing more opportunities for students to create media that can challenge problems, promote social/environmental justice, and enhance academics.

Lights, Sound, and Multimedia Action

Throughout the course, we guide students to experiment with media production by devoting separate classes to taking photographs (visual literacy), recording podcasts (aural literacy), and creating digital stories (multimedia literacy) that combine elements of visual and aural literacy. While these production skills could be taught as purely technical, we use the same sociocultural perspective and critical media literacy pedagogy to teach students about the potential of media production to challenge dominant ideologies and become tools for social change.

During the photography session, we explore many concepts of visual literacy, as well as experiment with cameras as pedagogical resources for the classroom. We engage with photographic theory and practical applications as we have students collaboratively create a list of photographic techniques by analyzing different magazine covers of the same person (Share, 2015b). For the photography assignments, teams of students use the list of photographic techniques that they just generated to illustrate select vocabulary words with their cell phone cameras. When they return with their photographs, students try to guess each other's words. Then they leave again to create the *good photo/ bad photo* assignment, in which they photograph the same person twice, to make them look good in one photo and bad in the other. After the police killing of Michael Brown, an unarmed African American teen in Ferguson, Missouri, hundreds of African Americans used Twitter to pose the question: if they gunned me down, which picture would the media choose? Using the hashtag #IfTheyGunnedMeDown, they tweeted pairs of pictures of themselves, usually one in which they looked more "socially acceptable" by commercial media standards and another in which they looked less "respectable" to the dominant media gaze (Vega, 2014). This is a powerful example of how the *good photo/ bad photo* assignment can have serious political implications as we see a new generation combining photography and social media to protest and challenge hegemony.

Using our ears and mouth more than our eyes, we explore the engineering of sound in media. Starting with a single phoneme, we practice pronouncing the letter O with different intonations to convey various meanings. Then we combine letters to spell the word *bad* and practice saying it differently to convey opposite meanings, from "not good" to "fabulous!" Next, we put words together and read the same sentence several times with different punctuation each time. These are skills students should learn for analyzing and creating different types of audio recordings. They are also useful for students learning to read and for English language learners, as they explore the ways words can change meaning simply by their pronunciation.

From words to sounds and music, we move into tone painting and explore how music conveys thoughts and emotions. After listening to short clips of famous musical scores, we discuss the role that music plays to tell stories, create atmosphere, and sometimes perpetuate stereotypes. These align with the visual and performing arts content standards for California public schools in all the categories: artistic perception, creative expression, historical and cultural context, aesthetic valuing, and connections, relationships, and applications.

Another engaging aspect of aural literacy is the use of sound effects. It can be highly motivating when students create their own sound effects while reading books or making movies. During this class, we bring in household items for students to experiment with, making sounds and listening to the feelings and images they evoke. In teams, students create podcasts with their cell phones in which they re-tell a media text or discuss a topic in a specific radio genre, using all the elements of aural literacy that were just covered.

During another session, we combine aural skills with visual literacy for students to create digital stories. There are numerous tools for making digital stories, but since most of our students teach in under-resourced inner-city schools, we teach them how to create a digital story with the most common computer program they are likely to find, Microsoft Office's PowerPoint. Many people are not aware that PowerPoint contains the option to record narration, something that can easily provide the soundtrack for a digital story. This is by no means the best program to use for making digital stories, but it is the most likely tool they will have access to and one of the programs they and their K-12 students are probably already somewhat familiar with using. Finding a tool that is accessible is important, but the tool is just a means for the most important work of learning how to tell a story.

We teach the basic elements of digital storytelling, show examples, and have students storyboard their ideas for creating a counter-hegemonic digital story (Ohler, 2008). In order to provide an easy and quick example that our teachers can take right into their classrooms, we have them use six index cards on which to draw the key scenes of their story. Students work in teams, distributing the tasks for drawing the illustrations, writing the script, recording the sound, and assembling all the elements in PowerPoint. Each digital story is first storyboarded and written as a script. The scenes are drawn horizontally on index cards that are then photographed, and the images are uploaded into a PowerPoint presentation. Finally, the group records their narration, dialogue, and sound effects. By creating their digital stories together in class, students are able to practice with each other the process that they can later use with their students.

Challenges for Creating Social Justice Educators

Most students find the use of media and popular culture to be excellent tools for discussing deep feelings and systemic structures of oppression, and yet some students are not ready or interested in delving into issues of racism, sexism, homophobia, and the systems and privileges that perpetuate them. Laura Ixta, a pre-service elementary school teacher, writes in her final course reflection that she was exposed to many new ideas, "and although sometimes I did get uncomfortable with the material presented, it is something that allowed me to explore why it made me uncomfortable. It allowed for self-reflection, and more learning about my own upbringing, my own experiences, and my own identity" (Ixta, 2014). These topics might not be necessary to implement the CCSS, but they are necessary if one is to be a social justice educator and work for transformative pedagogy. Critical media literacy aims to empower teachers and students with a sense of civic responsibility to confront social problems with progressive solutions, often involving media and technology. Our goal is to prepare teachers to be able to use technology and media to improve their teaching, as well as support social justice educators with ideas and strategies to inspire their students to action. High school science teacher John Choi (2013) writes in his final reflection for Ed466 about his experience bringing critical media literacy into his advisory class:

> In an organic manner, certain students had shifted from asking questions and examining media to seeking action. Questions of "what values are represented in the message" made way for questions that asked how we could change this problem. What I found was that social justice came from them and not my own urging; once they understood the injustice, students found themselves wanting to enact change. This powerful model of praxis, in which students took critical media literacy theory and called forth action, showed a pedagogy that had not been present in my advisory class before.

Choi's reflection is a powerful example of social justice education; however, not all of the projects that students complete articulate such a critical perspective.

While some of these experiences may lack the critical analysis that we aim for, we recognize that learning is a process involving different paths for different people; sometimes we are planting seeds and sometimes just opening doors. Critical media literacy pedagogy is intended to encourage students to explore popular culture, media, and technology through asking the questions that hopefully will guide them to more critical understandings of their world. Giroux (1987) writes:

> It is important to stress that a critical pedagogy of literacy and voice must be attentive to the contradictory nature of student experience and voice and therefore establish the grounds whereby such experience can be interrogated and analyzed with respect to both their strengths and weaknesses. (p. 20)

Democratic pedagogy requires non-judgmental dialectical struggle to question possible implications and consequences of all ideas and actions. The notion of a pedagogy that builds on theory and real-world experiences of students is a crucial component for thinking about how to incorporate critical media literacy into any content area or grade level (Morrell et al., 2013).

Twenty-first-century critical media literacy pedagogy integrates discussions of media representation, power, and ideology into a class instead of teaching this content as something separate. This is neither merely educational technology nor just a collection of lesson plans; it is a pedagogy that should serve as a framework to guide teachers and students to critically question all information, tools, and ideas. Reflecting on the course, elementary pre-service teacher, Julia Hiser (2012) explains that critical media literacy pedagogy:

> gives us, as teachers, a framework and a tool kit. We are equipped with the means to teach meaningful and relevant literacy, to foster critical awareness, to empower through production, and all in a way in which form matches content, in which the methodology of teaching mirrors the ideals of what is being taught.

Teacher education programs, like most K-12 public education in the US, are under considerable fire from people wanting to privatize all things public and from neoliberal policies requiring greater accountability to empirically prove effectiveness based on standardized high-stakes test scores. Flores-Koulish (2006) asserts, "The longer US public education's 'accountability movement' continues, the less our teachers have opportunities to engage students deeply in creative, original thought" (p. 239). Accompanying this drive for positivist notions of accountability and standardization are the Common Core State Standards that, on one hand, limit and homogenize what is to be taught, while on the other hand, open the door for an expanded understanding of literacy, the integration of more technological tools and media, and the empowerment of "students as critical thinkers through media production and analysis" (Moore & Bonilla, 2014, p. 7). In an educator's guide about the CCSS and media literacy published by the National Association for Media Literacy Education (NAMLE), Moore and Bonilla argue that "media literacy educa-tion...supports many of the most challenging goals of the Common Core State Standards" (p. 1).

Teachers act as role models, and the more media literate the teacher, the more likely the students will see an adult model critical thinking when it comes to discussions about popular culture, media, and technology. Goetze, Brown, and Schwarz (2005) stress that an important reason for teaching media literacy in teacher education programs is that "teachers cannot teach what they have not learned, and learned to value, themselves" (2005, p. 161). Therefore, to pre-pare teachers to bring critical media literacy into their classrooms they need to become media literate themselves and they also need to be prepared with a framework and pedagogy to guide their students to critically question and cre-ate alternatives to the messages they are seeing, hearing, and using every day.

CHAPTER 5

Environmental Justice Is Social Justice

In the 21st century, we are not only seeing exponential growth in digital technology and global connectivity, we are also experiencing record-breaking temperatures of the hottest days ever recorded around the world: "17 of the 18 warmest years since modern record-keeping began have occurred since 2001" (Sengupta, 2018). Climate conditions and extreme weather events during 2018 eroded climate change skepticism in some quarters and forced news media reports to finally start mentioning links between extreme weather and climate change (Lin & Panzar, 2018; Rubin, 2018). This is a significant shift, as even during 2016, the hottest year on record, the major TV networks (ABC, CBS, NBC, and FOX News) spent 66% less time covering climate change in 2016 than they did in 2015 (Kalhoefer, 2017). This decrease in reporting about climate change led to a combined total of just 50 minutes of news coverage for the entire year on that topic. Less than one hour of reporting about climate change for a year that included: the hottest temperatures ever recorded, the signing of the Paris climate agreement, numerous severe weather events, and a major presidential election with candidates voicing opposing views about the environment. Antonio López (2014) asserts, "Crucially, mass media play an instructional role by defining the status quo, setting the agenda for our socio-economic system, defining what to think about, and recursively reinforcing non-sustainable cultural beliefs" (p. 72). What media post, publish, and broadcast, or choose not to report, has significant consequences; and when they do decide to tell the story, how they frame it and explain it matters greatly.

As climate change becomes the biggest crisis to affect life on this planet, we are seeing corporations and politicians spinning facts and emotions to create doubt about the science and reframe the discourse. Neoliberal ideology, unregulated capitalism, rampant consumerism, sensationalized journalism, and the extraction and burning of fossil fuels are combining to create an environmental catastrophe that is changing everything (Klein, 2014). The media messages about these issues are an ideal space for students to critically analyze and challenge the assumptions, actions, and inactions. Using a framework of critical media literacy (CML), educators can guide students to question and create their own media messages about environmental justice and sustainability.

To encourage students to use their critical capacity, imagination, and creativity to explore and respond to climate change, educators need to break from the confines of the printed page and unleash the potential that lies beyond the

© KONINKLIJKE BRILL NV, LEIDEN, 2019 | DOI: 10.1163/9789004404533_005

margins. By incorporating ideas from CML, we can enhance students' reading and writing skills with all types of texts (movies, music, videogames, photographs, social media, books, etc.), deepen their understanding about the power of literacy, and stoke their creative spirits to learn about, as well as challenge, dominant narratives regarding our relationship with the natural world.

With the popularity and accessibility of cell phones and new mobile devices, youth are communicating and socializing every day in numerous ways, such as texting, tweeting, tagging, blogging, posting, pinning, instant messaging, photographing, podcasting, and sharing all types of texts. It is significant that the introduction to the Common Core State Standards specifically mentions the need for students to read and write with digital texts and "use technology and digital media strategically and capably" (Common Core State Standards, 2015, p. 7). According to a report by The National Environmental Education and Training Foundation (2005), "children get more environmental information (83%) from the media than from any other source" (Coyle, p. x). Since social media, smartphones, and the Internet have become the dominant conveyors of information and students' preferred option for communication and entertainment, teachers should be integrating these tools and practices into the classroom with theory and pedagogy that supports critical thinking.

In *Greening Media Education: Bridging Media Literacy with Green Cultural Citizenship*, López (2014) explains that there are many people in environmental education who think "media and technology are anti-nature" and that "the general practice of media literacy marginalizes ecological perspectives" (p. 1). However, it does not have to be this way. CML can be an important framework for uniting information communication technologies (ICTs) with environmental justice. Even though media education has not always supported sustainable practices and environmental perspectives, critical media literacy provides the potential to make education more transformative because it promotes social and environmental justice through critiquing dominant ideologies.

Teaching students to think critically about the messages they read, hear, see, and create requires an understanding of what it means to be literate in the 21st century that is inclusive of all types of information and entertainment. It is important to recognize the potential and limitations technology and media bring to education, especially for developing a critical engagement with environmental issues because many neoliberal education reforms support using technology and media to improve the efficiency and effectiveness of non-critical practices. Too often computers, cameras, and cell phones are used as fancy new tools to make the same old teaching practices just *look* better. However, when media, technology, and popular culture are embraced through CML pedagogy, there is far greater potential for education to become truly critical and empowering.

For decades, informal science education has worked with a deficit perspective and failed to promote critical thinking. A one-way transmission model, known as the Public Understanding of Science approach (PUS), has not been effective at educating the public about the seriousness of climate change (Cooper, 2011). The PUS approach is giving way to the Public Engagement in Science (PES) model of education that is more in line with CML because it supports critical thinking and an inquiry model of questioning. Caren Cooper argues, "In order to be climate change literate, the public must first be media literate" (p. 235). She writes:

> Science education efforts must be strategic and must expand courageously to provide the public with the critical thinking and media literacy skills that will help people recognize the barrage of media messages constructed to mislead, confuse, or predispose individuals to apathy or denial when engaging in dialogues about climate change. (p. 235)

While the PES model is an improvement over the more traditional "banking" approach, it does not prepare people to interrogate messages, to question dominant ideologies that shape assumptions, to recognize the influence of the medium through which information passes, and to see through the myth of neutrality to identify the economic structures that support commercial media. By using the CML framework of conceptual understandings and questions, educators can guide students to analyze media messages along with the structures and systems that support and influence them.

While much of the commercial media accessed on TV, radio, cell phones, and the Internet may seem free, it is important to recognize that they are economically dependent on advertising, which, in turn, needs endless consumption. Our consumerist ideology requires what Lewis and Boyce (2009) state is a "need to acknowledge the role that advertising plays in *creating a set of cultural conditions* that makes us less inclined to deal with climate change" (p. 8), and we would add, all environmental crises. Naomi Klein (2014) argues that we must change the consumption economic system through "de-growth" reductions. Executive Director of Greenpeace USA, Annie Leonard agrees with the need to change our unsustainable dependence on consumption and consumerism and calls for transformational solutions that will change our economic goals. In the online video, *Story of Solutions* (https://tinyurl.com/y7r2wo9m), Leonard explains that in order to make real changes to the system, we need to change the game and we can do this by shifting the goal from working for "more" stuff to working toward "better" solutions that will improve the quality of life for everyone (Leonard, Sachs, & Fox, 2013).

Klein (2014) asserts that social justice and environmental justice are profoundly interdependent:

> the climate moment offers an overarching narrative in which everything from the fight for good jobs to justice for migrants to reparations for historical wrongs like slavery and colonialism can all become part of the grand project of building a nontoxic, shockproof economy before it's too late. (p. 154)

Klein encourages us to understand climate change less as a single issue and more as a frame for seeing how all the problems that colonialism, imperialism, capitalism, and neoliberalism have been causing around the world are only going to become worse as temperatures rise.

For years, environmental problems in the US have been represented in mainstream media as issues of *universal vulnerability*, as if everyone were affected equally by environmental dangers. This hid the fact that low-income neighborhoods, especially communities of color, have been impacted with far worse consequences of environmental hazards than middle and upper class areas. Kate Aronoff (2018) writes, "People of color in the United States are *far more likely* to live near coal-fired power plants and suffer the associated health effects, and live in places where heavy weather hits hardest, thanks to years of targeted disinvestment in things like housing and infrastructure." When one takes into consideration issues of age, along with class and race, it becomes very apparent that the inequality of the effects of climate change put poor children of color on the front line. Frederica Perera (2016) reports, "While air pollution and the adverse health impacts of climate change affect us all, they are most damaging to children, especially the developing fetus and young child and particularly those of low socioeconomic status, who often have the greatest exposures and least amount of protection." The effects of climate change are also worse for people living on islands like the Maldives where rising sea levels are causing increasing flooding and putting the entire nation at risk (Berge, Cohen, & Shenk, 2011). Students need to understand that climate change is a problem that affects everyone, but not equally.

Another trope, often repeated in commercial media, is the notion of *universal responsibility*; the idea that we are all equally responsible for the environmental damages. While it is important that everyone feel a sense of responsibility and desire to improve the environment, it is also essential that corporations, governments, non-sustainable economic practices, and unjust ideologies be held accountable for the majority of the harm they are causing to the environment. In the August 1, 2018 issue of the *New York Times Magazine*, the entire magazine is dedicated to Nathaniel Rich's article, "Losing Earth: The Decade We Almost Stopped Climate Change." This in-depth analysis of climate change and public debate and action provides an excellent narrative of growing critical awareness of the accelerating dangers of climate change, but assigns blame and ascribes agency largely to individuals rather than seeing the complex interplay of individuals, corporations, the media, government, and social movements. Rich fails to address the idea that not everyone is equally responsible for the crisis we are now facing. Aronoff (2018) points out that Rich's article does not hold the fossil fuel companies or the largest carbon emitters to task:

> The numbers on this point are fairly clear: Just 100 companies have been responsible for 71 percent of emissions since 1988. According to a 2015 study from Oxfam, the poorest half of the world's population accounts for just 10 percent of emissions; around half stem from the richest 10 percent. That should inculpate the world's most carbon-hungry citizens – Those who fly often, for instance – but suggests a more nuanced picture than the old *Pogo* cartoon: "We have met the enemy, and he is Us."

The nations in the northern hemisphere have emitted far more CO_2 into the atmosphere than the countries currently experiencing the worst effects of global warming. Rich's suggestion that there may be something innately wrong with human nature moves the blame from economic structures, corporate greed, and systemic wealth inequality, to blame all humans. In the epilogue Rich writes, "We can trust technology and the economics. It's harder to trust human nature" (p. 66).

During a heyday for the environmental movement in the 1970s, one of the classic environmental commercials was known as the "Crying Indian," created by an organization called *Keep America Beautiful* (KAB). This popular television commercial is fraught with problems, from the actor playing the Native American actually being Italian American to the organization funding the ads being more concerned with selling beverages and packaging than environmental change. With the tagline, *People start pollution. People can stop it*, this one commercial reframed the public discourse in the US from corporate environmental devastation to a litter campaign in which all Americans can fight environmental pollution simply by picking up their trash (Dunaway, 2015). Teachers can download this commercial from YouTube (http://tinyurl.com/cye6k5l) and have their students answer the six CML questions after watching the commercial several times. Encouraging multiple viewings helps scaffold deep reading to uncover elements that are often missed the first time, such as the influence of sounds, editing, and considerations of what is missing. It is also helpful for students to critique media by considering the historical, cultural, and social contexts from when the texts were created, disseminated, and how they can be interpreted today in our own contemporary context. This commercial provides an example of how a non-profit organization can sponsor manipulative messages that seem positive on the surface, while working to undermine genuine change. KAB continues to promote litter campaigns at teacher education conferences and online, instead of encouraging their corporate members to change unsustainable business practices.

News Reporting on Environmental Problems

News reporting on science issues is often hampered by conventions of commercial journalism. In his popular book, *Bad Science*, Ben Goldacre (2009) points out that most journalists are graduates of the Humanities and thereby have less training in math and science methodologies and content. "They are also there to make money, to promote products, and to fill pages cheaply, with a minimum of journalistic effort" (Goldacre, p. 226). While many journalists produce excellent investigative reporting, the economic structures of commercial journalism unfortunately create systems that tend to prioritize profit over journalistic integrity (McChesney, 2004, 2015). The practice of publishing and broadcasting corporate-created press releases and video press releases without attribution has been increasing as media corporations merge and cost saving measures cut the funding and personnel necessary for original reporting (see FAIR's website for numerous examples: https://fair.org/). Another problem with commercial media's economic model is the culture of spectacle that favors sensationalism over in-depth analysis (Kellner, 2003).

One challenge with media representations of environmental issues is what Rob Nixon (2013) describes as the problem of "slow violence." Much of news media and movies appeal to audiences through sensationalizing momentary visual spectacles as dramatic entertainment. However, what is rarely portrayed is the slow violence:

> that is neither spectacular nor instantaneous but instead incremental, whose calamitous repercussions are postponed for years or decades or centuries...Stories of toxic buildup, massing greenhouse gases, and accelerated species loss because of ravaged habitats may all be cataclysmic, but they are scientifically convoluted cataclysms in which casualties are postponed, often for generations. (Nixon, 2011)

As a result, climate change gets inadequate coverage, as evident in an analysis of CNN's coverage during a week in 2015 that experienced record-breaking temperatures when they aired five times more oil industry advertising than coverage of climate change (Kalhoefer, 2016). Nixon (2013) notes the lack of media representation of "slow violence" is particularly evident in poor Southern Hemisphere countries such as Ecuador where there are few, if any, regulations on oil drilling, or the building of a dam in Brazil that displaced 40,000 mostly indigenous people and flooded 200 square miles of forests – furthering deforestation of Brazil.

Media stories about climate change are under-reported and when they are represented in mainstream media, they tend to be sensational and controversial. Researchers Leiserowitz and Smith (2017) investigated people's associations of the words "climate change" and "global warming" and report:

> One of the most important findings was what was not found – almost no respondents associated global warming with impacts on human health. Instead global warming was interpreted as a risk largely affecting non-human nature (e.g., ice and polar bears) far away in space and time and removed from the daily concerns of most people...

This suggests that many people still consider climate change as a distant problem that does not affect them, making it easier to ignore. Seldom are commercial media messages helpful to understanding the complexity of climate change in a way that motivates people to care and act. Analysis of TV news coverage of climate change by ABC, CBS, NBC, and Fox, found that they devoted only 146 minutes to climate change, despite the Paris climate summit, the EPA's Clean Power Plan, Pope Francis's papal encyclical, and other 2015 stories with the focus largely on extreme weather events and few, if any, references to impacts on national security, health, or economic growth (Media Matters for America, 2016). Most of the reporting provided a false balance related to framing the issue as debatable or controversial. There is also wide variation across media outlets in the degree of media coverage of climate change. Analysis of reporting of climate change between 2000 and 2015 by the *Washington Post*, *Wall Street Journal*, *New York Times*, *USA Today*, and *Los Angeles Times*, found that the *Wall Street Journal* and *USA Today* had consistently little or minor reporting while the *New York Times* and *Los Angeles Times* had far more coverage, particularly from 2007 to 2010 and then again in 2015 (Daly et al., 2015).

Finis Dunaway (2015) writes, "Yet, even as media images have made the environmental crisis visible to a mass public, they often have masked systemic causes and ignored structural inequalities" (p. 2). Students can do their own investigations about current media coverage. They can conduct quantitative research by counting the number of articles and news broadcasts on climate change and also qualitative research by evaluating the bias and construction of the reporting. *Fairness & Accuracy in Reporting* (FAIR) (http://fair.org) is a non-profit organization that provides regular critiques of media coverage in articles and in their podcast *CounterSpin* that can be useful for students to study specific examples of news reporting through a critical lens.

The fact that some news media and politicians still question the science of climate change makes the need for a media literate populace more essential than ever. While the debate in the scientific community ended decades ago, the popular discourse in commercial media is heavily influenced by public relations companies receiving large amounts of money from the fossil fuel industry (Oreskes & Conway, 2010). For students swayed by this deception, there are many resources available to critique climate deniers and triangulate the vast amount of scientific evidence. There are also resources to support teachers to guide their students to critically analyze the news, such as: Project LookSharp's (2010) *Media Construction of Global Warming: A Media Literacy Curriculum Kit,* The National Center for Science Education's website and resources *Dealing with Denial* (http://tinyw.in/BDkI) and the *Scientific Trust Tracker* (http://tinyw.in/meMw).

It is essential that students adopt a critical stance, given the history of the fossil fuel industry's covering up of information on the adverse effects of fossil fuels. Beginning in the 1970s, the fossil fuel industry launched a public relations campaign to silence or censor even the companies' own scientists' warning about emissions effects, as well as provided support for scientists who voiced denials regarding human causes of climate change (Oreskes & Conway, 2010). They also lobbied Congress and state legislators to oppose adding subsidies for alternative clean energies, and fought against a carbon fee or tax as proposed by the Citizens Climate Lobby (http://citizensclimatelobby.org).

As soon as Donald Trump was sworn into office in 2016, government officials were already changing the language and disappearing vital information about the environment from federal websites. The words "climate change" and "greenhouse gases" were often deleted or replaced with the terms "sustainability" and "emissions" (Environmental Data and Governance Initiative, 2018, p. 3). Web pages and links to data were removed or hidden, making it much more difficult to access information about climate change, environmental research, and the Obama administration's *Clean Power Plan* (Davenport, 2018). According to a report from the Environmental Data and Governance Initiative (2018):

> It is important to emphasize that EDGI's website monitoring efforts have thus far found *no removal or deletion of climate data sets from federal*

websites under the Trump administration. Instead, we have found substantial shifts in whether and how the topic of climate change and efforts to mitigate and adapt to its consequences are discussed across a range of federal agencies' websites. Perhaps most importantly, we have found significant loss of public access to information about climate change. (p. 8)

Arctic researcher, Victoria Herrmann (2017), argues that the disappearance of links to information such as statistics about Arctic permafrost thaw and maps of America's worst polluters, "undermine our ability to make good policy decisions by limiting access to scientific evidence." These changes to federal websites sparked concern from numerous scientists, archivists, and hackers around the world and led them to organize hackathons, "to capture the information from websites of the EPA, NASA, National Oceanic and Atmospheric Administration, and the United States Geological Survey" (Hansen, 2017). Organizations such as DataRefuge and the EDGI, along with concerned individuals, have been uploading this data to university servers and the Internet Archive (https://archive.org/index.php). EDGI researchers, Morgan Currie and Britt Paris (2018) explain four ways in which "climate-related information has become less accessible... (1) documents are difficult to find, (2) web pages are buried, (3) language has been altered, and (4) science has been silenced." Control of access to information is putting at risk essential requirements for democracy, the progress of consensus-based science, and the future of life on this planet. Learning about archives and the skills to access information have become new literacy competencies that students need in the digital age.

In 2017, the Heartland Institute, a conservative think tank, sent 300,000 unsolicited copies of a book full of misinformation about climate change to science teachers throughout the US. The 135-page book, *Why Scientists Disagree About Global Warming,* and accompanying DVD, is full of misleading claims, logical fallacies, and cherry-picked data based mostly on citations from their own people (Kelly, 2017). Curt Stager (27 April, 2017), professor of natural sciences explains, "The book is unscientific propaganda from authors with connections to the disinformation-machinery of the Heartland Institute." Strategic propaganda campaigns like this, focused on schoolteachers and funded by conservative think tanks with ties to the fossil fuel industry, require CML skills so students and teachers can deconstruct and make sense of the facts. A powerful CML activity could involve students using the six CML questions to compare and contrast the Heartland Institute publication with *The Teacher-Friendly Guide to Climate Change* published at the same time by the Paleontological Research Institute (Zabel, Duggan-Haas, & Ross, 2017). This activity can help students learn about the importance of climate change and also develop their critical thinking skills to analyze information. It is important that this inquiry delves beyond the idea that there are simply two different opinions on the topic, and instead investigates how propaganda functions by selecting and framing the facts, language, and sources that position the audience about what to think and believe.

Fake News and Climate Change

Recent interest in "fake news" can be an opportunity for students to think critically about media or it can be a dangerous ploy to confuse the public into thinking that there is just "fake news" contrasted to "real news." This false dichotomy tends to suggest that "fake news" is bad and "real news" is something we don't need to question because it is factual, objective, and THE whole truth. In between those two extremes lays much complexity and need for critical engagement with all information, communication, and entertainment.

The term "fake news" became popular during the 2016 election, when it was used to describe hoaxes that went viral. These were reports people created and disseminated for the intended purpose of fooling the public for political and/or economic gains, such as the fictitious Pizzagate and the false Papal endorsement of candidate Trump. The *New York Times* has called fake news, "a neologism to describe stories that are just not true," which they suggest has since been "co-opted to characterize unfavorable news" (Ember, 2017). Writing for *Common Dreams*, Neal Gabler (2016) provides a more critical analysis, arguing that fake news is an attack on truth that is intended "to destroy truth altogether, to set us adrift in a world of belief without facts, a world in which there is no defense against lies." It is important to consider who would benefit from a post-truth era in which science and facts are free for any interpretation. In the absence of accountability for facts or evidence, it is highly likely that those who control the airwaves and algorithms will define reality and truth as best fits their interests.

"Fake news" and "alternative facts" can be devastating to issues in which understanding observable facts and knowing scientific evidence is essential, such as anthropocentric climate change. For decades scientists have reported the data, facts, and evidence that human-caused CO_2 emissions are increasing the temperature of our planet. And yet, a small powerful group of individuals have managed to create doubt in public perceptions with unfounded claims that ignore the scientific evidence. This false notion of a controversy and uncertainty, as Naomi Oreskes and Erik Conway (2010) describe in their book, *Merchants of Doubt*, is not simply misinformation, it is actually a well-organized campaign of disinformation. When the President of the United States makes claims that are obviously false and completely unsubstantiated (such as crowd sizes, illegal voting, wiretapping, and climate change denials), he challenges the power of truth and honesty that the rule of law is based on. When media outlets repeat and disseminate these lies, they contribute to undermining a key foundation of democracy. These are actions that if unchecked, and allowed to continue, can only benefit those in power by allowing them to choose the versions of reality that best meet their political and financial interests.

The most dangerous "fake news" being repeated in commercial media, social media, and now government-sponsored media, is the denial of human-caused climate change. Fossil fuel companies have already spent billions buying rights to drill for oil and gas all over the world, something that will be devastating to our planet if it is allowed to continue. These multibillion-dollar corporations stand to lose large amounts of money if they do not adapt their practices as countries shift to renewable energy. Even though extracting and burning fossil fuels has been proven to be the primary cause of global warming, these corporations are spending less of their fortunes on switching to cleaner renewable energy and more on trying to convince people that climate change is fake. This challenge to the truth could not be more important at this point to determine the fate of human civilization.

Therefore, we are calling for an educational commitment to critical media literacy as an essential tool to empower students to critically question media and dominant ideologies, such as unregulated capitalism, overconsumption, fossil fuel dependency, and human exploitation of nature. Students at all grade levels can learn to search for truth through accessing multiple sources, triangulating different data, and making informed decisions based on facts, evidence, and research. Critical media literacy can help educators and students see through the smoke screen of "fake news" and "alternative facts" to learn the truth about climate change and take action before it is too late.

Creating Media to Challenge the Problems

While social media and new technologies are often contributing to the problem, it is important to remember that they can also be tools we can use to create solutions. Using humor and political satire to challenge the problematic way commercial media have framed climate change as an equal debate between two opposing positions, John Oliver (2014) challenges the imbalance in reporting by providing his own "mathematically representative climate change debate" (https://tinyurl.com/k5uslqx). During this episode of *Last Week*

Tonight, Oliver invites three climate change deniers to debate 97 scientists and visually demonstrates the problem with disproportionate reporting. This problem of "false balance" when reporting on climate change was addressed by the BBC in 2018 when they sent their journalists guidelines for how to report on climate change. The BBC policy states, "To achieve impartiality, you do not need to include outright deniers of climate change in BBC coverage, in the same way you would not have someone denying that Manchester United won 2–0 last Saturday. The referee has spoken" (Rosane, 2018).

During the 2016 Summer Olympics in Rio de Janeiro, ExxonMobil aired a deceptive television commercial that portrayed an environmentally conscious company, "powering the world responsibly" (https://tinyurl.com/j5lmm2x). In response to this attempt at greenwashing Exxon's image, ClimateTruth.org created a parody video that exposes the hypocrisy of Exxon's claims by remixing the same music and style of the original commercial with additional text that challenges their assertions of environmental responsibility (https://tinyurl.com/yd92h3no). Sharing these two short videos with students can be a powerful way to engage youth in critically analyzing media messages about the environment and the role of fossil fuel companies in contributing to the problems of climate change. The Climatetruth video can also be an excellent example of how students can become adbusters themselves and create their own media to challenge misleading attempts by industry and government to greenwash reality and deny the science about anthropomorphic climate change.

The Power of Visual Imagery

In 1968, a photograph from the darkness of space, showing a blue planet Earth rising over the moon, vitalized the environmental movement. Images of birds covered with tar from oil spills and baby seals being clubbed to death on ice floes, outraged the public and triggered emotional responses; even if only momentarily, they viscerally tugged at the heartstrings in a way that only photographs can. Viewing these pictures differently impacted people's attitudes and willingness to take actions. Images of climate change effects, such as aerial views of flooding, led many people to believe that climate change is important (O'Neill, Boykoff, Niemeyer, & Day, 2013). At the same time, these images actually undermined some people's sense of self-efficacy that they could address climate change, while other images, portraying energy futures, enhanced feelings of optimism and empowerment.

Teachers can find numerous images and visual presentations about climate change on the Internet (see http://climatechangeela.pbworks.com). There are a variety of sources today for students to see the visual effects of climate change, such as the time-lapse photography by James Balog in which he shows and discusses the results from his *Extreme Ice Survey* in his TED Talk online (Balog, 2009) and in the documentary *Chasing Ice* (Pesemen, Aronson, & Orlowski, 2012). NASA has several movies and interactive tools online that visually demonstrate the effects of climate change, such as the *Climate Time Machine, Global Ice Viewer, Images of Change, Eyes on the Earth 3D,* and other programs that allow users to move their cursor and see changes on planet Earth over time (http://tinyw.in/orCD). The Climate Reality Project provides infographics that simplify complex ideas with images and few words, making it an excellent tool for English language learners and all visual learners (*Telling the Story: Eight Great Infographics on Climate Change,* http://tinyurl.com/hokjbhf).

One of the best ways to teach students to read visual imagery is through creating visual images and teaching critical visual literacy (Kellner, 2002). The production process can be an ideal method for students to demonstrate their understanding of environmental justice and share their concerns with others. There are numerous websites to help students make their own infographics and visual thinking maps, such as Piktochart (http://piktochart.com) or Glogster (http://tinyw.in/h4Xr). Educational Technology and Mobile Learning's website lists 18 free programs for creating mind maps (http://tinyurl.com/7luyqeb).

Fedora Schooler, Middle School English/Social Studies Teacher

In her seventh grade English/Social Studies class in East Los Angeles, Fedora Schooler taught an 8-week unit combining critical media literacy with climate change. She began by showing students a hoax made by the BBC (Jones, 2008) of flying penguins that looks so real and is told in the documentary genre that most students did not question its authenticity and became convinced that penguins could fly. However, once they saw the backstory about how the BBC faked the images of flying penguins and created the hoax (BBC, 2008), they returned to their previous beliefs that penguins cannot fly. One student exclaimed, "in one minute we believed something as fact, then with one video we changed our minds." This activity captivated the students' interest about the manipulative potential of media and the desire to not be fooled again.

Schooler taught her students about critical media literacy and had them practice using the key questions that support the conceptual understandings. Students watched the movie *Wall-E* (Morris & Stanton, 2008) and analyzed the film from multiple perspectives applying the CML questions. Schooler explains, "when you are using these questions you need to frontload them with multiple opportunities to practice using them with different media." She also gave students a homework assignment to use the questions while watching commercials or any type of media.

To learn the scientific facts about climate change, students read informational texts and watched videos such as: Leonardo DeCaprio's 2016 Oscar acceptance speech, Balog's (2009) TED Talk on *Time Lapse Photography of Extreme Ice Loss*, Bill Nye the Science Guy, and a BrainPop animation. They also annotated an informational text about climate change from their school Science textbook, then re-read it to create Cornell notes. To organize the information, they used Thinking Maps: multi-flow maps (for cause and effects), tree maps (for categorizing) and a bubble map (for describing). After learning about the science, Schooler had her students create environmental justice posters that conveyed information about climate change on one sheet of paper with an image and brief text. In order to make appropriate decisions about their choice of words, images, and design of their poster, students referred to the CML questions throughout the creation process.

Encouraging students to collaborate and discuss their ideas, Schooler separated her class into teams to read different picture books and view various media that address environmental issues. She had a heterogeneous group of mixed reading levels in which some struggling readers were unable to decode and/or comprehend grade-level texts. By using high quality picture books and multimedia texts (such as: spoken word video, TV commercial, online art exhibit, and animated cartoons), all the students had access to the content to be able to reflect critically and participate fully in the discussions. After critiquing the messages and the mediums of their various texts, students dressed up in costumes and made oral advertising pitches for their books and movies using language arts techniques of persuasion.

Schooler integrated this unit with poetry by having her students read Robert Frost's *The Road Less Traveled*. They discussed the elements of poetry and considered how the poem relates to their discussions about climate change. Students made personal connections, such as, "right now we are at the part of the road where we have to make a decision. Should we help stop climate change or should we continue burning fossil fuels and cutting down trees until we destroy the entire environment?"

For their final project, student groups chose various environmental issues that they were most drawn to and worked collaboratively to create some type of media that combined images and words in order to present their information to their peers. The class generated a large list of possible media projects based on all the different items they could think of in which images and words are used together, such as: food packaging, posters, movies, animation, t-shirts, menu, etc. One group re-purposed the food package of Nutella as a way to address the issue of deforestation as companies exploit palm oil to make Nutella. They created a new packaging label with information about the environmental impact that corporate farming of palm oil is having on the forests in Indonesia. One group made a t-shirt and another made a poster to address problems of global warming and the role of fossil fuels to accelerate climate change. A comic strip was created by one team that investigated lead contamination of the water in Flint, Michigan and problems of ammonia in the water in Los Angeles. Schooler reflects:

> During this unit my students became aware of the possibility of manipulation by the media and how to better recognize and analyze the media's influence in their lives. Through studying climate change, they learned that their actions have impact on the world, and that media can be used to positively spur change.

Nick Kello, Elementary School Music Teacher

At the University of California, Los Angeles (UCLA) Lab School, music teacher Nick Kello taught a unit about climate change and music to all the students in grades 3–6 to help them understand the role music has played and continues to play in social movements, especially environmental issues. Kello organized the unit around the guiding question, "what can music tell us about the way in which different human societies have related to their natural environment?" Through focusing his students on this question, Kello used music as a lens to understand the relationships between humans and nature. He began by reading aloud the book, *Brother Eagle, Sister Sky*, in which Susan Jeffers provides an adaptation of the famous speech by Chief Seattle from the 1850s.

While there is controversy about the actual words that Seattle spoke, this literature provided an entry point for Kello's students to reflect on the relationships humans have had with nature and to question the current ideas students carry about their connections to the land, water, and sky. Kello had his students consider various Native American perspectives by listening to music from contemporary Chumash people living in Santa Barbara and Hopi snake dance rituals in Arizona. Students analyzed musical attributes, the meanings of the lyrics, and the ritualistic elements of the music. Often returning to the guiding question, Kello led his students to reflect on Native American relationships with nature, through art, music, and rituals.

The next genre Kello introduced was folk music by having students listen to different versions of Woody Guthrie's classic song, *This Land is Your Land*. Students analyzed various lyrics, purposes, and uses of the song and explored the ways music has been used to tell stories and question humans' relationship with nature. In one verse, Guthrie sings, "the wheat fields waving and the dust clouds rolling," which created an opportunity to examine the historical context of the American Dust Bowl. Kello showed students clips from Ken Burns' (2012) documentary, *The Dust Bowl* (available on PBS). Students learned about one of the worst man-made disasters in US history and were able to make connections between the greed and drought of the 1930s with the causes and effects of climate change today. Kello used music by Woody Guthrie as well as the following songs to help students explore the effects of manifest destiny, the industrial revolution, and humans' relationship to nature: *Big Yellow Taxi* by Joni Mitchell, *Where do the Children Play?* by Cat Stevens, and *Mercy, Mercy Me (The Ecology)* by Marvin Gaye.

Kello had previously worked with the students to learn various songs of protest. For this unit they focused on environmental songs and issues. Students watched news clips about climate change and the movie trailer for *The Island President* (http://theislandpresident.com/) to see how issues of climate change are not affecting everyone equally. Students learned about the water crisis in Flint, Michigan and even problems with contaminated water in downtown Los Angeles. Students also discussed climate change denial and US attitudes about climate change, comparing the way some politicians in the US still question the facts of climate change while most of the world has already accepted the scientific reality of it. After discussing science and politics, Kello showed students examples of how songs and music have been used in social movements to galvanize issues and bring people together. Kello explains that the very act of making music goes against individualism,

> music is inherently social, the idea that music is for entertainment is a social construction, music has historically been linked to social ritual, rite, or event, not in isolation. Music brings people together; it is inherently participatory, people dance, tap, and sing along. It allows people to share in a single experience together. It binds and unites people with ideas and feelings and actions together at the same time. Music can be an emotional experience for building community and solidarity.

In order to help students understand how various aspects of music work to position the audience to think and feel certain ways, Kello played for his students the popular theme song, *Everything is Awesome*, from *The Lego Movie*

(2014). He began by having students listen to the song with questions on the board for them to consider: "what is the emotional quality of the song, what is the instrumentation, and what does this have to do with climate change?" Having no background knowledge about the song's relationship to climate change, the students were intrigued to discover the connection. Kello showed them a music video created by Greenpeace (https://www.youtube.com/watch?v=CM_HFLIsaKo) that uses the same song slowed down, with harmonic alterations, and played over images of a pristine Lego Arctic filling-up with black oil to the point that only the Shell flag remains above the muck. The song and video were part of a political campaign to pressure the toy company to break its ties with the oil company, as the final tagline reads, "Shell is polluting our kids' imaginations. Tell Lego to end its partnership with Shell." Kello explains that when his students watched the Greenpeace video

> they were so blown away, they kept wanting to see it over and over again. It is just so powerful, we talked about how the tone painting totally changes, major chords are substituted for minor chords, the tempo is slowed down, but the words stayed the same. That created a total cognitive dissonance between the words, the imagery in the video, and the emotional tone painting of the music.

Since the goal of the Greenpeace video was to disrupt the decades-long relationship that Shell Oil has had with Legos toys, Kello showed his students a newspaper article about arctic drilling and a Lego set from the 1970s with a Shell gas station. They discussed the implications of this partnership and the dangers of drilling for oil in the Arctic. The students were fascinated with the way Greenpeace had used a popular song to fight against climate change, so when Kello finally told them how the Greenpeace video was seen by thousands of people and actually caused Legos to end their partnership with Shell Oil (Petroff, 2014), the students in every class jumped up and cheered. It was a powerful lesson that led wonderfully into the students creating their own climate change songs. They were inspired because this gave them the proof that music really can have an impact.

In order to show his students an example of somebody their own age using music to challenge the problems of climate change, Kello played the eco rap hip hop video of *Melting Ice* by Lil Peppi (http://tinyurl.com/hc4cbjx) (Hopkins, 2009). After preparing his students to understand the power of music for social change and the problems of climate change, Kello had them become music makers and work together to create their own songs that challenge climate change. Kello reviewed everything they had discussed throughout the unit about climate change and listed the issues as a way to remind them of the things they could include in their song. They also talked about solutions and students loved listening to Prince Ea's music videos, especially *Man vs Earth* (http://tinyurl.com/za3c20g), which concludes with suggestions for reforestation and real ways people can combat climate change. The lessons that Kello taught during the students' music class integrated well with the lessons they were learning during their other classes, especially the poetry writing they were doing in Language Arts. When they started writing song lyrics, Kello pointed out the similarities with writing poetry.

To write their songs, students first worked in pairs to compose two lines of a verse that had to rhyme and meet a specific number of syllables. Then pairs joined together into groups of four and reviewed each other's lines to create one four-line verse. They were writing and writing verses after verses. One example from a group of third graders:

> *Greenhouse gases are polluting the sky,*
> *Ocean levels are rising too high,*
> *People are cutting down too many trees,*
> *The birds are dying and so are the bees.*

Kello typed their words for each class to review and they democratically chose ten verses and one chorus. They ended with a set of lyrics and Kello downloaded several free rap beats from the Internet. He talked about using free beats that were open source, and had the students choose the beat that resonated most with them. They practiced rapping the lyrics with the beat and then recorded their final product. They also talked about what to do with the recordings. Time was tight at the end of the school year, so the students decided to continue with this the following year. They were excited to go public with their songs and share their music with the mayor, the president, friends, and family.

Incorporating music and aural texts to address environmental and social justice issues has tremendous potential to engage students who are often bored or feel excluded by traditional teaching practices. There are songs, like *Love Song to the Earth* (Gad, Shanks, Bedingfield, & Paul, 2015) featuring a collection of famous singers, who directly address climate change and provide a meaningful way for students more musically inclined to connect with environmental issues. For music created by youth, see the video of 13-year-old indigenous rights activist Xiuhtezcatl Martinez performing hip-hop about climate change (http://tinyw.in/qBbD). Students can discuss their responses and write analyses of songs (http://tinyw.in/nKcG) that are used or could be used in the climate change movement (for examples http://tinyw.in/w91F).

Students can also listen to podcasts such as the Commonwealth Club Climate One podcasts (http://tinyw.in/y9V1) that feature guests addressing various issues associated with climate change. Working together, students can create podcasts that allow their voices to be heard and provide counter-stories to challenge dominant narratives of race, class, gender, sexuality, or any topic they feel is being misrepresented or underrepresented (Bell, 2010). They can also submit their own "climate change stories" (http://tinyw.in/lmmA) for potential airing on the Climate Connect radio program (http://tinyw.in/WNsu) produced by the Yale Climate Communications project.

Using Digital Media to Participate in Civic Society

While adults may be accessing information about climate change through print or TV news outlets, young people are more likely to obtain their news through online social media outlets such as Twitter, Instagram, and YouTube (Anderson & Jiang, 2018; Newman, Fletcher, Levy, & Nielsen, 2016). Given the popularity of social media for sharing information and ideas, students can use social media platforms to communicate their perspectives on climate change. Through the use of Twitter, Facebook, Snapchat, Pinterest, and other platforms, students can share narratives and videos with hashtags describing their specific actions for fostering sustainability.

Adolescents are increasingly turning to digital media to voice their perspectives on issues, as documented in the book *By Any Media Necessary: The New Youth Activism* (Jenkins, Shresthova, Gamber-Thompson, Kligler-Vilenchi, & Zimmerman, 2016) and the book by Parkland Florida students David and Lauren Hogg (2018) *#Never Again. A New Generation Draws the Line*. Reports from the *Journal of Digital and Media Literacy* (http://www.jodml.org) suggest that the skills students are learning by using social media in their participatory culture are potential resources and strategies for their participation in political actions and collective activism (Jenkins et al., 2016).

Information communication technologies provide opportunities for youth and adults to connect, organize, and carry out actions to counter commercial media and politicians who are ignoring and/or denying the realities of climate science. Educators can be key players in this work, teaching students how to use literacy and technology to read and write the word and the world. Our students need role models and guides to facilitate their learning to understand and challenge dominant ideologies that are threatening their very future.

Using a critical media literacy framework of conceptual understandings and questions, educators can encourage their students to ask critical questions about the messages they are hearing and seeing in media all around them. CML is an inquiry process that applies to all aspects of our lives because we live in such mediated societies in which public discourse always reflects ideological values and perspectives. We must help students question and respond to the messages, systems, and structures that are supported by ideologies of over-consumption, toxic patriarchy, and savage capitalism that are putting our survivability at risk.

Teachers in all subjects can make their content more meaningful and relevant by engaging with popular culture and current events. Incorporating movies, TV, music, social media, news reports, video games, photographs, and all types of media can make classrooms more engaging for students growing up in our media-saturated environment. However, simply using more media is not sufficient. As the public is becoming more accustomed to the media spectacle with infotainment and "alternative facts," educators need to guide their students to think critically about information and entertainment, analyze its construction, and evaluate its effects. Critical media literacy can be an ideal pedagogy to support teachers and students in their struggle to make sense of the messages and to create their own alternative media that can challenge the myths and support the facts.

The time is ripe for students to become leaders capable of discerning spin from facts and empowered to use all types of media to promote sustainable practices and priorities to protect everybody's future.

CHAPTER 6

Concluding Thoughts

We have described the theoretical trajectories and practical applications of the knowledge, skills, and conceptual understandings that constitute critical media literacy. For over a decade, we have argued that in our digitally networked media age, "critical media literacy is not an option, it is an imperative" (Kellner & Share, 2007, p. 68). Throughout this book, we have discussed the need for a critical approach to literacy that questions ideological constructions of race, class, gender, sexuality, and other identity markers. Media education should prepare people to make sense of the information, communication, and entertainment we use and depend on daily in order to be able to participate in our democracy as informed citizens. We have provided examples of ways educators have used CML to question who benefits and who is harmed by media representations that normalize and reproduce racism, sexism, classism, homophobia, and other forms of discrimination.

In an age of global warming, continual warfare, economic crises, and humanitarian struggles across the globe, we cannot afford to passively consume media and trust corporations or governments to act in our own best interests. Critical media literacy is essential for a participatory democracy and the humanization of education because citizens must be able to make sense of the information, question the power, and challenge the social and environmental injustices that are threatening our very existence. This work should begin with the conceptual understandings of CML that have evolved from the knowledge that information is never neutral or objective.

Challenging the Myths of Neutrality and Objectivity

Challenging the ideological constructions of normality, neutrality, and the myth of objectivity, are among the key goals of CML which are often excluded or overlooked in much traditional education (Apple, 2004; Giroux, 1997; Kincheloe, 2007). CML pedagogy embraces education as a political act. Lewis and Jhally (1998) assert, "Media literacy should be about helping people to become sophisticated citizens rather than sophisticated consumers" (p. 1). Freire and Macedo (1987) explain:

> The myth of the neutrality of education – which leads to the negation of the political nature of the educational process, regarding it only as a task

> we do in the service of humanity in the abstract sense – is the point of
> departure for our understanding of the fundamental differences between
> a naive practice, an astute practice, and a truly critical practice. (p. 38)

Negating the political nature of education only supports the status quo and
conserves power structures, masking them as if they do not exist. Giroux (1997)
writes, "The notion that theory, facts, and inquiry can be objectively deter-
mined and used falls prey to a set of values that are both conservative and
mystifying in their political orientation" (p. 11). Through disrupting unexam-
ined beliefs about what is normal or natural, students unveil ideologies and
hegemonic structures that are all too often invisible (Hall, 2012; Kumashiro,
2000; Vasquez, 2014).

What many take for granted as "normal" today, was and is created within
formal hegemonic systems of power, as well as within informal commonplace
ideological discourses. The word "normal" is a relativist term that implies a
dominant standard in contrast to something "abnormal," or "unnatural." In
psychology, "normal" intelligence is given an IQ range of 90–110. In medicine,
a "normal" human body temperature is considered 98.6 degrees Fahrenheit.
The word "normal" is a misnomer for what is common or typical. What an
individual or a society deems "normal" is always a contextually-based decision
and not universal or inherently obvious to everyone at all times. However, this
social construction is not usually considered when most people use the term
"normal." While there are beneficial uses of normative standards, and some
disciplines and activities depend on utilizing these standards, the assumption
that what is considered to be "normal" is neutral and apolitical must be challenged. This is especially important in the fields of medicine and psychology,
wherein the antonym of "normal" is "abnormal" and therefore warrants medical intervention, as homosexuality once did.

The construct of *normalcy* is neither innocent nor harmless, it often contributes to many layers of injustice hidden under a metaphorical baseline to which
most people become accustomed. When what is assumed to be "normal" veils
non-dominant perspectives, it hides or denies injustice. The normalizing of
patriarchy assumes male entitlement at the expense of female opportunity and
equal rights. The normalizing of heterosexual relationships entitles heterosexual partners to rights and privileges denied to non-heterosexual couples. While
these injustices are often more visible and palpable to people in subordinate
positions (such as women, LGBTQ folks, and people of color), it is typically the
overt acts of violence or extreme levels of injustice that enter the public discourse
and are reported in mainstream media. This is apparent in news reporting that
overlooks or downplays crimes *against* people of color while sensationalizing

violent crimes committed *by* people of color. When daily news reports normalize the idea that African-Americans are mostly the perpetrators of violent crime and not the victims, many Whites are more likely to internalize fears of African Americans, instead of developing empathy for the actual victims.

Systemic discrimination against women, people of color, low-income earners, religious minorities, LGBTQ individuals, and other marginalized groups is less visible today, but still continues to influence society and reproduce inequalities. While gender equality has increased since women got the right to vote, still fewer than one fourth of all political offices and titles are held by women (Rutgers, 2014). Further, studies of the predominance of male producers, directors, writers, and industry workers over women in the entertainment industry show that women are subordinate throughout a wide spectrum of positions, jobs, and roles in the media (Hunt, Ramón, Tran, Sargent, & Roychoudhury, 2018).

Similarly, discrimination against people of color in the US is also accompanied by underrepresentation and misrepresentations of them in media. While the statistics of incarceration and school suspension among Blacks could be used to highlight the shameful state of race relations in America today, they are instead often exploited by media to attract audiences and increase profit. When compared to Whites, Blacks are six times more likely to be incarcerated during their lifetimes (NAACP, 2014). Furthermore, "Black students represent 18% of preschool enrollment but 42% of students suspended once, and 48% of the students suspended more than once" (United States Department of Education, 2014). Compounding these problematic statistics is the rate at which Blacks are portrayed as criminals on televised news, twice as often as Whites, who continue to outnumber Blacks in prison (Chiricos & Eschholz, 2002). Media representations are never neutral; they often amplify disparities to sensationalize facts and gain broader audiences (Duncan, 2012; Iyengar & Kinder, 1987; Krosnick & Kinder, 1990).

These statistics and media portrayals are neither coincidences nor evidence of the inferiority of women, the work ethic of Blacks, or the mental stability of LGBTQ individuals. Instead, they reveal systemic injustices: a media-saturated society that regularly repeats these hegemonic representations will be more likely to think of politicians as male, Blacks as criminals, and transgender individuals as freaks. All of these representations begin to establish a baseline of what a culture considers "normal." Establishing this baseline of normalcy, media (whether purposefully or inadvertently) accustom their viewers/readers/listeners to see White, heterosexual males as the model of normalcy and the rightful possessors of power; yet rarely name or identify them as beneficiaries of privilege. Johnson (2006) points out that "privileged groups are also usually taken as the standard of comparison that represents the best society has to offer" (p. 95). He explains, that these "privileged groups are assumed to represent society as a whole, 'American' is culturally defined as white, in spite of the diversity of the population. This is evident in a statement like 'Americans must learn to be more tolerant of other races'" (p. 96).

CML interrogates the myth of objectivity by examining the systems (e.g. canons, ideologies, philosophies, structures, laws, and organizations) that are often presumed to be neutral because of a deeply buried history of power and dominance, which goes unmarked and unmentioned. By using CML concepts and questions, students learn to scrutinize the systems and processes that make media representations and networked communicative acts appear "normal" or "natural."

CML pedagogy is rooted in the premise that no text or medium can be free of bias or completely neutral because communication is a subjective process. Even the mathematical algorithms that drive search engines are not neutral (Noble, 2018). Media messages and the medium they travel through are created and emerge from a cultural milieu that may advertise itself as "neutral" (or objective) when in actuality, it consistently privileges dominant groups. Depending on the context and who has power, privileged perspectives may include ablest, capitalist, cisgender (those living in accordance with their gender assignment from birth), property-owners, Protestant, and the list continues depending on whose perspective is privileged enough "to disappear from view into the taken-for-granted 'naturalised' world of common sense" (Hall, 2003, p. 90). The United States, founded on the belief that only land-owning White males could vote, has changed considerably since its founding, and yet wealthy White males are still granted unearned privileges at the expense of women, people of color, and the poor.

With new media and social networking enabling people to increasingly engage in processes of participating and constructing realities, so too can systemic injustices that have routinely passed as "normal" be exposed. Media production is an important part of CML because often students are unaware of privileged and disadvantaged perspectives until they create narratives, art, and digital media that affirm their own unique perspectives. The process of enabling students to construct digital media and give a voice and/or visual representation to their experiences that challenge what is often considered "normal" can be educational and empowering.

Fostering Democracy and Global Citizenship

In the early 20th century, John Dewey argued that democracy requires educated citizens and that schools should promote education for citizenship and participation in democratic processes. Critical Media Literacy aims to advance goals of democracy, justice, and citizenship, yet in an increasingly networked world, a critical and transformative pedagogy should teach students to think about their roles as social justice-oriented citizens in their communities, nations, and globalized world. In *Educating the "Good" Citizen: Political Choices and Pedagogical Goals,* Westheimer and Kahne (2004) call on educators to examine their concepts of citizenship and citizenship education. Calling attention to a lack of social justice education in the curriculum, Westheimer and Kahne (2004) point to the California Department of Education's restriction on schools from participating in activism, advocacy, lobbying, and marches to celebrate Cesar Chavez Day (p. 244). Teachers and students are encouraged to celebrate the individual achievements of Cesar Chavez (California Department of Education, 2014), as if he operated outside of the social context of history, without the support of countless activists, and isolated from other struggles for civil and human rights. Educators must be cognizant of the kind of citizenship they promote through their pedagogy, because "the choices we make have consequences for the kind of society we ultimately help to create" (Westheimer & Kahne, 2004, p. 265). Indeed, what is omitted from a curriculum can be more significant than that which is included, because increasing students' exposure to a broad range of perspectives and experiences is integral to promoting social justice and what Ferguson (2001) calls "critical solidarity."

Critical solidarity involves recognizing the interconnections between people and information as well as demonstrating empathy to be in solidarity with those marginalized or oppressed by these connections (Ferguson, 2001). As the proliferating media landscape increasingly shapes students' culture, it is imperative for educators to understand how media engagement will soon be synonymous with civic engagement, and how this engagement can be utilized to foster critical solidarity. This means teaching students to interpret information and communication within humanistic, social, historical, political, and economic contexts so they begin to understand the interrelationships and consequences of their actions and lifestyles. It also means joining in solidarity, or global citizenship, with the disempowered in a collective struggle for a more just world. Many of these ideas are being promoted internationally by organizations like United Nations Educational, Scientific, and Cultural Organization (UNESCO) and the European Commission. However, in the US, few reform initiatives promote this type of pedagogical change (Gozálvez & Contreras-Pulido, 2014).

For two decades, UNESCO (2014) has championed the importance of establishing peace "on the basis of humanity's moral and intellectual solidarity." To this aim, UNESCO has been researching media education, holding international conferences, and publishing reports that encourage the international community to embrace media literacy. It now promotes media education that is intimately linked to global citizenship. In 2006, UNESCO published a media education kit in Arabic, English, and French (Frau-Meigs, 2006), and in 2011, it published a *Media and Information Literacy Curriculum for Teachers* in ten different languages (Grizzle & Wilson, 2011). Commissioned by UNESCO, Tornero and Varis (2010) investigated digital and media literacy to develop a conceptual framework, which they published in their book, *Media Literacy and New Humanism*. Tornero and Varis (2010) argue that educators need to move beyond an instrumental view of digital literacy, to one with an essential critical component necessary for students to inquire into:

> the *reasons* why we interpret media texts with a given bias or orientation; the *mechanisms* through which media communicate *world views, points of view, beliefs and ideologies,* that is, a kind of culture, which they do in a stealthy, silent way, as if they were not doing it, as if their discourse were transparent. (p. 96)

Tornero and Varis (2010) assert, "universal global citizenship is synonymous with media literacy for all" (p. 119). Framing this as an economic and civic necessity, they conclude that the ultimate value of media literacy is peace. "This means accepting the elementary principle that no one is right without dialogue and there is no peace without freedom and justice" (Tornero & Varis, 2010, p. 126).

Some Latin American and Spanish media educators call for "educommunication," an interdisciplinary combination of the academic fields of education and communication. Gozálvez and Contreras-Pulido (2014) assert that educommunication "has a civic purpose, that is, it must be endowed with an ethical, social and democratic base that empowers citizens in their dealings with the media" (p. 130). Educommunication calls for global citizenship that includes multiple notions of civic engagement. "It is a call to a certain condition: to be an independent being in possession of freedom, acting with responsibility and as a protagonist in the various spheres or dimensions of public life" (Gozálvez & Contreras-Pulido, 2014, p. 130).

Pioneer of media literacy, Len Masterman (1996), asserts that media literacy is necessary to assure human rights. He describes three generations of human rights: the first generation rights are civil and political rights, second generation are economic and social rights, and the third generation are communication rights. The communication rights include *information rights*, which cover the right to find, get, and deliver ideas and information; the *right to communicate,* addresses the expressive rights to exchange information and speak out to make one's voice heard; and *media rights,* include the rights of access and use of the media, something which implies "a number of *media responsibilities* in terms of content, representation, access, control, accountability and training," according to Masterman (1996, p. 73).

However, communication rights are dependent on a public that is or will become media literate. Because of this educational need, Masterman suggests that a fourth generation of human rights should be added, called "interpretive rights: the rights of access to those skills and discourses which will enable citizens and future citizens to interpret, make their own sense of, and produce their own meanings from the media" (p. 74). He insists that these interpretive rights are not only necessary for communicative rights, but in today's media-saturated world, interpretive rights are essential for first and second generation human rights as well. Therefore, interpretive rights are a mandate for the spread and implementation of media education. Masterman writes that interpretive rights also help focus media literacy to "aspire to be an effective education in human rights" (p. 74). He insists that of all the concepts of media literacy, the most important concept to link the function and role of media with issues of human rights is the concept of representation.

Challenging under-representations or misrepresentations in media can be a powerful place for students to engage in social activism, a necessary component to participatory democracy. Some CML teachers ask students to analyze stereotypical representations of gender, ethnicity, and class in music videos, online games, or questionnaires, while others work with students on interactive projects that engage students in community outreach and Youth Participatory Action Research (YPAR). Hence, education for democracy and social justice requires students to question media and create alternative representations that challenge media underrepresentation and misrepresentations.

While the CCSS provides some windows of opportunity for the inclusion of CML throughout the curriculum, it continues to promote equality as synonymous with equity and education as non-political. If we merely teach students the skills they will need to find a job, then we will miss engaging them in truly transformative education. CML supports 21st century literacy skills essential for careers, college, and much more. CML is a transformative pedagogy that offers a solid theoretical base and practical teaching methodology to critically empower students to question their world and challenge the dominant myths that seem "normal" or "natural." Today's students need the skills and guidance to critically question and create their world.

Students today live in a space less defined by binaries and absolutes, and more open to adaptation, diversity, and innovation. Studies in feminism,

LGBTQ issues, human rights, critical race theories, environmental justice, and globalization have encouraged students to be more aware of the complexity of identities and issues. However, along with this openness to diversity has arisen a relativist sentiment, which risks the loss of critical judgment, and promotes an apolitical perspective that everything is equal and everyone deserves to be heard no matter how racist, sexist, classist or hateful the message. While CML encourages tolerance of difference, it does not subscribe to relativistic notions that all ideas are equal and every perspective is valid. Instead, CML takes a strong critical stance against racism, sexism, classism, homophobia, and other forms of discrimination that are often reinforced by mainstream media.

In this book, we have described concepts, pedagogical practices, and questions that support critical inquiry and provide a framework and methods for critically engaging with the most influential ecosystem humans have created. CML calls for critical inquiry into the hierarchical power relations that are embedded in all communication and ultimately benefit some at the expense of others. Critical media literacy provides a theoretical framework and transformative pedagogy to empower students to question media, challenge dominant ideologies, and participate in society as critical and active media users and creators. How teachers, students, and citizens will engage and practice critical media literacy will differ in various contexts and situations, yet the construction of critically informed media producers, critics, and users remains a major pedagogical and political challenge of our time.

References and Resources

Anderson, M., & Jiang, J. (2018). *Teens, social media & technology 2018*. Pew Research Center: Internet and Technology.

Apple, M. (2004). *Ideology and curriculum* (3rd ed.). New York, NY: Routledge.

Aronoff, K. (2018, August 2). What the "New York Times" climate blockbuster got wrong. *The Nation*. Retrieved from https://www.thenation.com/article/new-york-times-climate-blockbuster-misses/

Arrows, F. (2013). *Teaching truly: A curriculum to indigenize mainstream education*. New York, NY: Peter Lang.

Asante-Muhammad, D., Collins, C., Hoxie, J., & Nieves, E. (2017). *The road to zero wealth: How the racial wealth divide is hollowing out America's middle class*. Washington, DC: Institute for Policy Studies & Prosperity Now. Retrieved from https://www.prosperitynow.org/files/PDFs/road_to_zero_wealth.pdf

Atkinson, W. (2010). *Class, individualization and late modernity: In search of the reflexive worker*. New York, NY: Palgrave Macmillan.

Balog, J. (2009). *Time-lapse proof of extreme ice loss* [Video file]. TEDGlobal 2009. Retrieved from http://tinyurl.com/pqq5u64

Banks, J. (2000). Series forward. In C. Cortés (Ed.), *The children are watching: How the media teach about diversity*. New York, NY: Teachers College Press.

Banta, M., & Hinsley, C. M. (1986). *From site to sight: Anthropology, photography, and the power of imagery*. Cambridge, MA: Peabody Museum Press.

Barthes, R. (1981). *Camera lucida: Reflections on photography*. New York, NY: Noonday Press.

BBC. (2008, April 1). *Making penguins fly on April Fools' day 2008* [Video file]. British Broadcasting Corporation. Retrieved from https://www.youtube.com/watch?v=lzhDsojoqk8

Beach, R. (2009). Digital tools for collecting, connecting, constructing, responding to, creating.... In R. Hammer & D. Kellner (Eds.), *Media/cultural studies: Critical approaches* (pp. 206–228). New York, NY: Peter Lang.

Beach, R., Share, J., & Webb, A. (2017). *Teaching climate change to adolescents: Reading, writing, and making a difference*. New York, NY: Routledge. (Co-distributed with NCTE).

Bell, L. A. (2010). *Storytelling for social justice: Connecting narrative and the arts in anti-racist teaching*. New York, NY: Routledge.

Benshoff, H. M., & Griffin, S. (2009). *American on film: Representing race, class, gender, and sexuality at the movies*. Malden, MA: Wiley-Blackwell.

Berge, R., Cohen, B. (Producers), & Shenk, J. (Director). (2011). *The Island President* [Motion Picture]. New York, NY: Samuel Goldwyn Films.

Berr, J. (2018, November 5). NBC, Fox, Facebook yank Trump immigration ad critics call racist. *Forbes Online*. Retrieved from https://tinyurl.com/y7fv8orb

Best, S., & Kellner, D. (2001). *The postmodern adventure: Science technology, and cultural studies at the third millennium*. New York, NY & London: Guilford and Routledge.

Bigelow, B., Christensen, L., Karp, S., Miner, B., & Peterson, B. (Eds.). (1994). *Rethinking our classrooms: Teaching for equity and justice*. Milwaukee, WI: Rethinking Schools.

Bogle, D. (1989). *Toms, coons, mulattoes, mammies, & bucks: An interpretive history of Blacks in American films*. New York, NY: Continuum.

Botelho, G. (2016). The day politics and TV changed forever. *CNN Politics*. Retrieved from https://www.cnn.com/2016/02/29/politics/jfk-nixon-debate/index.html

boyd, d. (2014). *It's complicated: The social lives of networked teens*. New Haven, CT: Yale University Press.

Brady, M. (2012, August 21). Eight problems with common core standards. *The Washington Post*. Retrieved from https://tinyurl.com/8fnjqjb

Britsch, S. (2010). Photo-booklets for English language learning: Incorporating visual communication into early childhood teacher preparation. *Early Childhood Education Journal, 38*(3), 171–177.

Buckingham, D. (1993). *Children talking television: The making of television literacy*. London: The Falmer Press.

Buckingham, D. (1996). *Moving images: Understanding children's emotional responses to television*. Manchester: Manchester University Press.

Buckingham, D. (2003). *Media education: Literacy, learning and contemporary culture*. Cambridge: Polity Press.

Burns, K. (Director). (2012). *The Dust Bowl* [Motion picture]. New York, NY: Public Broadcasting System.

Burton, N. (2015, September 18). *When homosexuality stopped being a mental disorder: Not until 1987 did homosexuality completely fall out of the DSM* [Blog post]. Retrieved from https://www.psychologytoday.com/us/blog/hide-and-seek/201509/when-homosexuality-stopped-being-mental-disorder

Butsch, R. (2003). Ralph, Fred, Archie, and Homer: Why television keeps re-creating the white male working-class buffoon. In G. Dines & J. M. Humez (Eds.), *Gender, race, and class in media: A text-reader* (2nd ed., pp. 575–585). Thousand Oaks, CA: Sage Publications.

Byard, S. (2012). *Combining African-centered and critical media pedagogies: A 21st-century approach toward liberating the minds of the mis-educated in the digital age* (Doctoral dissertation). Retrieved from ProQuest LLC. (UMI No. 3513191).

California Department of Education. (2014). *Model curriculum and resources for teachers*. Retrieved from http://chavez.cde.ca.gov/ModelCurriculum/Teachers/index1.aspx

Campbell, R., Jensen, J., Gomery, D., Fabos, B., & Frechette, J. (2013). *Media in society*. Boston, MA: Bedford/St. Martin's.

Cappello, M. (2011). Photography for teacher preparation in literacy: Innovations in instruction. *Issues in Teacher Education, 20*(1), 95–108.

Cappello, M., & Hollingsworth, S. (2008). Literacy inquiry and pedagogy through a photographic lens. *Language Arts, 85*(6), 442–449.

Carr, N. (2014). *The glass cage: How our computers are changing us.* New York, NY: W.W. Norton & Company.

Carrington, V. (2005). New textual landscapes, information and early literacy. In J. Marsh (Ed.), *Popular culture, new media and digital literacy in early childhood* (pp. 13–17). London: RoutledgeFalmer.

Castells, M. (1996). *The information age: Economy, society and culture, Volume 1: The rise of the network society.* Cambridge, MA: Blackwell Publishers.

Chesney, R., & Citron, D. (2018, February 21). Deep fakes: A looming crisis for national security, democracy and privacy? *Lawfare* [Blog post]. Retrieved from https://www.lawfareblog.com/deep-fakes-looming-crisis-national-security-democracy-and-privacy#

Ching, C. C., Wang, X. C., Shih, M. L., & Kedem, Y. (2006). Digital photography and journals in a kindergarten-first-grade classroom: Toward meaningful technology integration in early childhood education. *Early Education and Development, 17*(3), 347–371.

Chiricos, T., & Eschholz, S. (2002). The racial and ethnic typification of crime and the criminal typification of race and ethnicity in local television news. *Journal of Research in Crime and Delinquency, 39*, 400–420.

Choi, J. (2013, Fall). *EDUC 446: Critical media literacy final reflection.* Submitted as a final assignment for the course.

Colbert, S. (2009, July 16). *The word – White man's burden* [Video file]. Comedy Central's The Colbert Report. Retrieved from http://thecolbertreport.cc.com/videos/ttoy6c/the-word---neutral-man-s-burden

Collins, P. H. (2000). *Black feminist thought: Knowledge, consciousness, and the politics of empowerment* (2nd ed.). New York, NY: Routledge.

Common Core State Standards. (2015). *Common core state standards for English language arts & literacy in history/social studies, science, and technical subjects.* Common Core State Standards Initiative. Retrieved from http://tinyurl.com/kjgs8a5

Cooper, C. B. (2011). Media literacy as a key strategy toward improving public acceptance of climate change science. *BioScience, 61*(3), 231–237.

Cortés, C. (2000). *The children are watching: How the media teach about diversity.* New York, NY: Teachers College Press.

Coyle, K. (2005). *Environmental literacy in America: What ten years of NEETF/Roper research studies say about environmental literacy in the U.S.* National Environmental Education and Training Foundation. Retrieved from http://tinyurl.com/jk3jfkj

Crenshaw, K. (1991). Mapping the margins: Intersectionality, identity, politics, and violence against women of color. *Stanford Law Review, 43*(6), 1241–1299.

Currie, M., & Paris, B. S. (2018, March 21). Buried, altered, silenced: 4 ways government climate information has changed since Trump took office. *The Conversation*. Retrieved from https://theconversation.com/buried-altered-silenced-4-ways-government-climate-information-has-changed-since-trump-took-office-92323

Curtis, N., & Cardo, V. (2018). Superheroes and third-wave feminism. *Feminist Media Studies, 18*(3), 381–396.

Daly, M., Gifford, L., Luedecke, G., McAllister, L., Nacu-Schmidt, A., Andrews, K., & Boykoff, M. (2015). *World newspaper coverage of climate change or global warming, 2004–2015*. Center for Science and Technology Policy Research, Cooperative Institute for Research in Environmental Sciences, University of Colorado. Retrieved from http://sciencepolicy.colorado.edu/media_coverage

Daniels, M. (2013, January 8). *Scientific racism: The eugenics of social Darwinism. A documentary by David Olusoga for the BBC Four* [Video file]. Retrieved from https://www.youtube.com/watch?v=3FmEjDaWqA4

Darder, A., Baltodano, M., & Torres, R. (Eds.). (2003). *The critical pedagogy reader.* New York, NY: RoutledgeFalmer.

Davenport, C. (2018, January 10). How much has 'climate change' been scrubbed from federal websites? *The New York Times*. Retrieved from https://www.nytimes.com/2018/01/10/climate/climate-change-trump.html

DeGruy, J. (2005). *Post traumatic slave syndrome: America's legacy of enduring injury and healing*. Portland, OR: Joy DeGruy Publications.

Dewey, J. (1916/1997). *Democracy and education*. New York, NY: Free Press.

Dewey, J. (1938/1963). *Experience & education*. New York, NY: Collier Books.

Domine, V. (2011). Building 21st-century teachers: An intentional pedagogy of media literacy education. *Action in Teacher Education, 33*(2), 194–205.

Dragan, P. B. (2008). *Kids, cameras, and the curriculum: Focusing on learning in the primary grades*. Portsmouth, NH: Heinemann.

Duggan, M. (2013). *Photo and video sharing grow online*. Pew Research Center. Retrieved from http://www.pewinternet.org/2013/10/28/photo-and-video-sharing-grow-online/

Dunaway, F. (2015). *Seeing green: The use and abuse of American environmental images*. Chicago, IL: The University of Chicago Press.

Duncan, J. (2012). *Racial disparities associated with the war on drugs* (Master's thesis). Appalachian State University, Boone. Retrieved from http://www.libre.uncg.edu

Durham, M. G., & Kellner, D. (2006). *Media and cultural studies: Key works*. Malden, MA: Blackwell Publishers.

Ember, S. (2017, April 3). This is not fake news (but don't go by the headline). *New York Times, Education Life, EDTALK*. Retrieved from https://www.nytimes.com/2017/04/03/education/edlife/fake-news-and-media-literacy.html

Englander, E. K. (2011). *Research findings: MARC 2011 survey grades 3-12.* Bridgewater State University, Massachusetts Aggression Reduction Center. Retrieved from http://cdn.theatlantic.com/static/mt/assets/science/Research%20Findings_%20 MARC%202011%20Survey%20Grades%203-12.pdf

Environmental Data and Governance Initiative. (2018). *Changing the digital climate: How climate change web content is being censored under the Trump administration.* Retrieved from https://envirodatagov.org/wp-content/uploads/2018/01/Part-3-Changing-the-Digital-Climate.pdf

Ewald, W. (2012). Introduction. In W. Ewald, K. Hyde, & L. Lord. *Literacy & justice through photography: A classroom guide.* New York, NY: Teachers College Press.

Facebook Investor Relations. (2018, July 25). *Facebook reports second quarter 2018 results.* Menlo Park, CA. Retrieved from http://investor.fb.com/releasedetail.cfm? ReleaseID=861599

Ferguson, K. (n.d.). *Everything is a remix* [Video file]. Retrieved from http://everythingisaremix.info/watch-the-series/

Ferguson, R. (1998). *Representing 'race': Ideology, identity and the media.* New York, NY: Oxford University Press.

Ferguson, R. (2001). Media education and the development of critical solidarity. *Media Education Journal, 30,* 37–43.

Ferguson, R. (2004). *The media in question.* New York, NY: Oxford University Press.

Flax, J. (1997). Postmodernism and gender relations in feminist theory. In S. Kemp & J. Squires (Eds.), *Feminisms* (pp. 170–178). New York, NY: Oxford University Press.

Flores-Koulish, S. A. (2006). Media literacy: An entrée for pre-service teachers into critical pedagogy. *Teaching Education, 17*(3), 239–249. doi:10.1080/10476210600849706

Flores-Koulish, S. A., Deal, D., Losinger, J., McCarthy, K., & Rosebrugh, E. (2011). After the media literacy course: Three early childhood teachers look back. *Action in Teacher Education, 33,* 127–143.

Foucault, M. (1995). *Discipline and punish: The birth of the prison.* New York, NY: Vintage Books.

Frau-Meigs, D. (Ed.). (2006). *Media education: A kit for teachers, students, parents and professionals.* Paris: UNESCO. Retrieved from http://unesdoc.unesco.org/ images/0014/001492/149278e.pdf

Fregoso, R. L. (1993). *The bronze screen: Chicana and Chicano film culture.* Minneapolis, MN: University of Minnesota Press.

Freire, P. (2010). *Pedagogy of the oppressed* (M. B. Ramos, Trans.). New York, NY: The Continuum International Publishing Group, Inc. (Original work published 1970)

Freire, P., & Macedo, D. (1987). *Literacy: Reading the word and the world.* Westport, CT: Bergin & Garvey.

Friedman, T. L. (2005). *The world is flat: A brief history of the twenty-first century.* New York, NY: Farrar, Straus & Giroux.

Funk, S., Kellner, D., & Share, J. (2016). Critical media literacy as transformative peda-gogy. In M. N. Yildiz & J. Keengwe (Eds.), *Handbook of research on media literacy in the digital age* (pp. 1–30). Hershey, PA: IGI Global.

Gabler, N. (2016, November 30). Who's really to blame for fake news? Look in the mir-ror, America. *Common Dreams.* Retrieved from http://www.commondreams.org/views/2016/11/30/whos-really-blame-fake-news-look-mirror-america

Gad, T., Shanks, J., Bedingfield, N., & Paul, S. (2015). *Love song to the earth* [Recorded by Paul McCartney, Jon Bon Jovi, Sheryl Crow, Fergie, Colbie Caillat, Natasha Beding-field, Sean Paul, Leona Lewis, Johnny Rzeznik (Goo Goo Dolls), Krewella, Angelique Kidjo, Nicole Scherzinger, Kelsea Ballerini, Christina Grimmie, Victoria Justice, & Q'orianka Kilcher].

Galloway, S. (2017). *The four: The hidden DNA of Amazon, Apple, Facebook, and Google.* New York, NY: Portfolio/Penguin.

Gauntlett, D., & Hill, A. (1999). *TV living: Television, culture and everyday life.* London & New York, NY: Routledge.

Gee, J. (2007). *What video games have to teach us about learning and literacy: Revised and updated edition.* New York, NY: Palgrave Macmillan.

Gibbons, P. (2009). *English learners, academic literacy, and thinking: Learning in the challenge zone.* Portsmouth, NH: Heinemann.

Ging, D. (2017). Alphas, betas, and incels: Theorizing the masculinities of the manosphere. In *Men and masculinities* (pp. 1–20). Retrieved from http://journals.sagepub.com/doi/pdf/10.1177/1097184X17706401

Giroux, H. (1987). Introduction. In P. Freire & D. Macedo (Eds.), *Literacy: Reading the words and the world* (pp. 1–27). Westport, CT: Bergin & Garvey.

Giroux, H. (1997). *Pedagogy and the politics of hope.* Boulder, CO: Westview Press.

Giroux, H. (2004). When hope is subversive. *Tikkun, 19*(6), 38–39.

GLAAD Media Institute. (2018). *Where we are on TV '17-'18: GLAAD's annual report on LGBTQ inclusion.* Retrieved from https://www.glaad.org/whereweareontv17

Goetze, S. D., Brown, D. S., & Schwarz, G. (2005). Teachers need media literacy, too! In G. Schwarz & P. Brown (Eds.), *Media literacy: Transforming curriculum and teaching.* Malden, MA: The 104th Yearbook of the National Society for the Study of Education.

Goldacre, B. (2009). *Bad science.* London: Fourth Estate of HarperCollins Publishers.

Goldberg, S. (2018, April). To rise above the racism of the past, we must acknowledge it. From the Editor (pp. 4–6). *National Geographic Magazine.*

Goldberg, V. (1991). *The power of photography: How photographs changed our lives.* New York, NY: Abbeville Press.

González, N., Moll, L. C., & Amanti, C. (Eds.). (2005). *Funds of knowledge: Theoriz-ing practices in households, communities, and classrooms.* Mahwah, NJ: Lawrence Erlbaum Associates.

Goodman, S. (2003). *Teaching youth media: A critical guide to literacy, video production, and social change.* New York, NY: Teachers College Press.

Goodman, S. (2010). Toward 21st-century literacy and civic engagement: Facilitating student documentary projects. In J. G. Silin (Ed.), *High-needs schools: Preparing teachers for today's world* (pp. 44–54). New York, NY: Bank Street College of Education.

Gozálvez, V., & Contreras-Pulido, P. (2014). Empowering media citizenship through educommunication. *Comunicar, 21*(42), 129–136.

Graham, P. (2017). *Strategic communication, corporatism and eternal crisis: The creel century.* New York, NY: Routledge.

Graham, P. (in press/2019). Propaganda and public pedagogy. In G. Noblett (Ed.), *Oxford research encyclopedia of education.* Oxford: Oxford University Press.

Grieco, M. (Artist). (2012). *Media literacy's big tent* [image]. Retrieved from http://mediaeducationlab

Grizzle, A., & Wilson, C. (Eds.). (2011). *Media and information literacy: Curriculum for teachers.* Paris: UNESCO.

Habermas, J. (1984/1981). *Theory of communicative action volume one: Reason and the rationalization of society* (T. A. McCarthy, Trans.). Boston, MA: Beacon Press.

Hall, S. (1998). Notes on deconstructing 'the popular.' In J. Storey (Ed.), *Cultural theory and popular culture: A reader.* Upper Saddle River, NJ: Pearson/Prentice Hall.

Hall, S. (2003). The whites of their eyes: Racist ideologies and the media. In G. Dines & J. M. Humez (Eds.), *Gender, race, and class in media: A text-reader* (2nd ed., pp. 89–93). Thousand Oaks, CA: Sage Publications.

Hall, S. (2012). *Stuart Hall interviewed by Sut Jhally* [Video file]. Retrieved from http://vimeo.com/53879491

Hall, S. (2013). Introduction. In S. Hall, J. Evans, & S. Nixon (Eds.), *Representation* (2nd ed., pp. xvii–xxvi). Thousand Oaks, CA: Sage Publications.

Hansen, T. (2017, February 24). The student-built website that keeps government climate data safe. *Yes! Magazine.* Retrieved from http://www.yesmagazine.org/planet/the-student-built-website-that-keeps-government-climate-data-safe-20170221

Harding, S. (1998). *Is science multicultural? Postcolonialism, feminisms, and epistemologies.* Bloomington, IL: Indiana University Press.

Harding, S. (Ed.). (2004). *The feminist standpoint theory reader: Intellectual and political controversies.* New York, NY: Routledge.

Hartsock, N. (1997). The feminist standpoint: Developing the ground for a specifically feminist historical materialism. In S. Kemp & J. Squires (Eds.), *Feminisms* (pp. 152–160). Oxford: Oxford University Press.

Haskell, M. (1974). *From reverence to rape: The treatment of women in the movies.* Baltimore, MD: Penguin Books.

Hernstein, R., & Murray, C. (1994). *The bell curve: Intelligence and class structure in American life*. New York, NY: Free Press.

Herrmann, V. (2017, March 28). I am an Arctic researcher: Donald Trump is deleting my citations. *The Guardian*. Retrieved from https://www.theguardian.com/commentisfree/2017/mar/28/arctic-researcher-donald-trump-deleting-my-citations

Hiser, J. (2012, Fall). *EDUC 446: Critical Media Literacy Final Reflection*. Submitted as a final assignment for the course.

Hobbs, R. (2007). *Approaches to instruction and teacher education in media literacy*. Research paper commissioned within the United Nations Literacy Decade. UNESCO Regional Conferences in Support of Global Literacy.

Hobbs, R. (2010). *Copyright clarity: How fair use supports digital learning*. Thousand Oaks, CA: Corwin.

Hobbs, R. (2013). *Media literacy's big tent*. Retrieved from http://mediaedlab.com/2013/07/28/media-literacy-s-big-tent-at-namle-2013/

Hogg, D., & Hogg, L. (2018). *#Never again: A new generation draws the line*. New York, NY: Random House.

hooks, b. (2010). *Teaching critical thinking: Practical wisdom*. New York, NY: Routledge.

Hopkins, C. A. (2009). *Lil Peppi – Melting ice* [Video file]. Retrieved from https://www.youtube.com/watch?v=yjXuldy-Ilw

Howard, T. C. (2010). *Why race and culture matter in schools: Closing the achievement gap in America's classrooms*. New York, NY: Teachers College Press.

Hunt, D., Ramón, A. C., Tran, M., Sargent, A., & Roychoudhury, D. (2018, February). *Hollywood diversity report 2018: Five years of progress and missed opportunities*. UCLA College, Social Sciences. Retrieved from https://socialsciences.ucla.edu/hollywood-diversity-report-2018/

Iqbal, N. (2018, November 11). Interview: Donna Zuckerberg: "Social media has elevated misogyny to new levels of violence." *The Guardian*. Retrieved from https://tinyurl.com/y74lb6ph

Ixta, L. (2014, Spring). *EDUC 446: Critical media literacy final reflection*. Submitted as a final assignment for the course.

Iyengar, S., & Kinder, D. (1987). *News that matters*. Chicago, IL: University of Chicago Press.

Jenkins, H. (2006). *Convergence culture: Where old and new media collide*. New York, NY: New York University Press.

Jenkins, H., Shresthova, S., Gamber-Thompson, C., Kligler-Vilenchi, N., & Zimmerman, A. M. (2016). *By any media necessary: The new youth activism*. New York, NY: New York University Press.

Johnson, A. (2006). *Privilege, power, and difference* (2nd ed.). New York, NY: McGraw-Hill.

Jones, T. (2008, March 31). *Penguins – BBC* [Video file]. British Broadcasting Corporation. Retrieved from https://www.youtube.com/watch?v=9dfWzp7rYR4

Kalhoefer, K. (2016, April 25). *Study: CNN viewers see far more fossil fuel advertising than climate change reporting* [Blog post]. Retrieved from http://tinyw.in/SZcr

Kalhoefer, K. (2017, March 23). *How broadcast networks covered climate change in 2016* [Blog post]. Retrieved from https://tinyurl.com/yb4kyfcs

Katz, J. (2006). *The macho paradox: Why some men hurt woman and how all men can help*. Naperville, IL: Sourcebooks, Inc.

Kellner, D. (1989). *Critical theory, Marxism, and modernity*. Cambridge & Baltimore, MD: Polity Press and John Hopkins University Press.

Kellner, D. (1995). *Media culture: Cultural studies, identity and politics between the modern and the postmodern*. New York, NY: Routledge.

Kellner, D. (2002). Critical perspectives on visual literacy in media and cyberculture. *Journal of Visual Literacy, 22*(1), 3–12.

Kellner, D. (2003). *Media spectacle*. New York, NY: Routledge.

Kellner, D. (2005). *Media spectacle and the crisis of democracy*. Boulder, CO: Paradigm Press.

Kellner, D. (2010). *Cinema wars: Hollywood film and politics in the Bush/Cheney era*. Malden, MA: Blackwell Publishers.

Kellner, D. (2016). *American nightmare: Donald Trump, media spectacle, and authoritarian populism*. Rotterdam, The Netherlands: Sense Publishers.

Kellner, D. (2017). *The American horror show: Election 2016 and the ascendency of Donald J. Trump*. Rotterdam, The Netherlands: Sense Publishers.

Kellner, D., & Share, J. (2007). Critical media literacy, democracy, and the reconstruction of education. In D. Macedo & S. R. Steinberg (Eds.), *Media literacy: A reader* (pp. 3–23). New York, NY: Peter Lang.

Kelly, S. (2017, June 17). US senators deem Heartland Institute mailings to grade school science teachers "possibly fraudulent." *Truthout.org*. Retrieved from https://truthout.org/articles/us-senators-heartland-institute-mailings-to-grade-school-science-teachers-possibly-fraudulent/

Kessler, G. (2018, December 11). Meet the Bottomless Pinocchio, a new rating for a false claim repeated over and over again. *The Washington Post*. Retrieved from https://tinyurl.com/ybt7pgbo

Kilbourne, J. (2010). *Killing us softly 4: Advertising's image of women* [Video file]. Northampton, MA: Media Education Foundation.

Kim, K. (2013, December). *Kiyun Kim: Racial microaggressions* [Online photographic exhibit]. Retrieved from http://nortonism.tumblr.com/

Kincheloe, J. (2007). *Critical pedagogy primer*. New York, NY: Peter Lang.

Klein, N. (2014). *This changes everything: Capitalism vs. the climate*. New York, NY: Simon & Schuster.

Kolb, L. (2008). *Toys to tools: Connecting student cell phones to education*. Eugene, OR: ISTE.

Kovach, B., & Rosenstiel, T. (2011). *Blur: How to know what's true in the age of informa-tion overload*. New York, NY: Bloomsbury.

Krashen, S. (1992). *The input hypothesis: Issues and implications*. Laredo, TX: Laredo Publications.

Krosnick, J., & Kinder, D. (1990). Altering the foundations of support for the president through priming. *American Political Science Review, 84*(2), 497–512.

Kumashiro, K. (2000). Toward a theory of anti-oppressive education. *Review of Educa-tional Research, 70*(1), 25–53.

Lauredhel. (2007, April 29). *Passive aggression: Foregrounding the object* [Blog post]. Retrieved from https://hoydenabouttown.com/2007/04/29/passive-aggression-foregrounding-the-object/

Leiataua, A. (2013, Winter). *EDUC 446: Critical media literacy final reflection*. Submitted as a final assignment for the course.

Leiserowitz, A., & Smith, N. (2017). Affective imagery, risk perceptions, and climate change communication. In E. von Storch (Ed.), *Oxford research encyclopedia of cli-mate science*. Oxford: Oxford University Press.

Leonard, A., Sachs, J. (Writers), & Fox, L. (Director). (2013). *The story of solutions: Why making real change starts with changing the game* [Video file]. Free Range Studios. Retrieved from http://storyofstuff.org/movies/the-story-of-solutions/

Lewis, J., & Boyce, T. (2009). Climate change and the media: The scale of the challenge. In T. Boyce & J. Lewis (Eds.), *Climate change and the media* (pp. 1–16). New York, NY: Peter Lang.

Lewis, J., & Jhally, S. (1998). The struggle over media literacy. *Journal of Communication, 48*(1), 1–8.

Lin, R-G., II, & Panzar, J. (2018, August 5). Record heat in California is no fluke, experts warn: Rising temperatures have fueled wildfire conditions and blunt talk from sci-entists about climate change. *Los Angeles Times*, p. A1.

López, A. (2014). *Greening media education: Bridging media literacy with green cultural citizenship*. New York, NY: Peter Lang.

Lowen, J. W. (1999). *Lies across America: What our historic sites get wrong*. New York, NY: The New Press.

Ludwig, M. (2014, May 20). Everything you ever wanted to know about the FCC's net neutrality proposal. *Truthout*. Retrieved from http://truth-out.org/news/item/23820-everything-you-ever-wanted-to-know-about-the-fccs-net-neutrality-proposal

Luke, A., & Freebody, P. (1997). Shaping the social practices of reading. In S. Muspratt, A. Luke, & P. Freebody (Eds.), *Constructing critical literacies: Teaching and learning tex-tual practice* (pp. 185–225). Sydney: Allen & Unwin, and Cresskill, NJ: Hampton Press.

Luke, A., & Freebody, P. (1999). Further notes on the four resources model. *Reading Online*. Retrieved from https://pdfs.semanticscholar.org/a916/0ce3d5e75744de3d0ddacfaf6861fe928b9e.pdf

Luke, C. (1990). *Constructing the child viewer: A history of the American discourse on television and children, 1950–1980*. New York, NY: Praeger.

Luke, C. (2000, February). New literacies in teacher education. *Journal of Adolescent and Adult Literacy, 43*(5), 424–436.

Marx, K., & Engels, F. (1970). *The German ideology*. New York, NY: International Publishers.

Marx, K., & Engels, F. (1978). *The Marx-Engels reader*. New York, NY: Norton.

Masterman, L. (1985/2001). *Teaching the media*. New York, NY: Routledge.

Masterman, L. (1996). Media education and human rights. *Continuum: The Australian Journal of Media & Culture, 9*(2), 73–77.

McChesney, R. W. (2004). *The problem of the media: U.S. communication politics in the twenty-first century*. New York, NY: Monthly Review Press.

McChesney, R. W. (2015). *Rich media, poor democracy: Communication politics in dubious times*. New York, NY: The New Press.

McLuhan, M. (1962). *The Gutenberg galaxy: The making of typographic man*. Toronto: University of Toronto Press.

McLuhan, M. (2003). *Understanding media: The extensions of man: Critical edition* (T. Gordon, Ed.), Berkeley, CA: Gingko Press.

Media Matters for America. (2016). *How broadcast networks covered climate change in 2015: An analysis of nightly news and Sunday shows*. Retrieved from https://tinyurl.com/y9egc75s

Mendoza, L. (2016, Spring). *EDUC 446: Critical Media Literacy Final Reflection*. Submitted as a final assignment for the course.

Mihailidis, P. (2008). Are we speaking the same language? Assessing the state of media literacy in U.S. higher education. *Studies in Media & Information Literacy Education, 8*(4), 1–14.

Monarrez, N. (2017). *Critical media literacy and its effects on middle school students' understandings of different perspectives* (Unpublished master's inquiry project). University of California, Los Angeles, CA.

Moore, D. C., & Bonilla, E. (2014). *Media literacy education & the common core state standards: NAMLE an educator's guide*. National Association for Media Literacy Education. Retrieved from https://namleboard.files.wordpress.com/2015/04/namlemleccssguide.pdf

Morrell, E. (2012). 21st Century literacies, critical media pedagogies, and language arts. *The Reading Teacher, 66*(4), 300–302. doi:10.1002/TRTR.01125

Morrell, E., Dueñas, R., Garcia, V., & López, J. (2013). *Critical media pedagogy: Teaching for achievement in city schools*. New York, NY: Teachers College Press.

Morris, J. (Producer), & Stanton, A. (Director). (2008). *Wall-E* [Motion Picture]. Disney Pixar.

Mulaudzi, S. (2017, January 25). Let's be honest: Snapchat filters are a little racist. *Huffington Post* (Edition ZA). Retrieved from https://www.huffingtonpost.co.za/2017/01/25/snapchat-filters-are-harming-black-womens-self-image_a_21658358/

NAACP. (2014). *Criminal justice fact sheet.* Retrieved from http://www.naacp.org/pages/criminal-justice-fact-sheet

Naureckas, J. (2018, May 15). Media can tell readers who's killing whom – When they want to. *Fairness & Accuracy in Reporting.* Retrieved from https://fair.org/home/media-can-tell-readers-whos-killing-whom-when-they-want-to/

NCTE. (2008). *Code of best practices in fair use for media literacy education.* National Council of Teachers of English Position Statement. Retrieved from http://www.ncte.org/positions/statements/fairusemedialiteracy

New London Group. (1996). A pedagogy of multiliteracies: Designing social futures. *Harvard Educational Review, 66*(1), 60–92.

Newman, N., Fletcher, R., Levy, D. A. L., & Nielsen, R. K. (2016). *Reuters Institute digital news report 2016.* New York, NY: Reuters. Retrieved from http://tinyw.in/AaiB

Nixon, R. (2011, June 26). *Slow violence* [Blog post]. Retrieved from http://tinyw.in/zEt5

Nixon, R. (2013). *Slow violence and the environmentalism of the poor.* Cambridge, MA: Harvard University Press.

Noble, S. U. (2012, Spring). Missed connections: What search engines say about women. *Bitch, 54,* 36–41.

Noble, S. U. (2013, October). Google search: Hyper-visibility as a means of rendering black women and girls invisible. *InVisible Culture,* 19. Retrieved from http://ivc.lib.rochester.edu/google-search-hyper-visibility-as-a-means-of-rendering-black-women-and-girls-invisible/

Noble, S. U. (2018). *Algorithms of oppression.* New York, NY: New York University Press.

Norton, B. (2015, October 5). Media are blamed as US bombing of Afghan hospital is covered up. *Fairness & Accuracy in Reporting.* Retrieved from https://fair.org/home/media-are-blamed-as-us-bombing-of-afghan-hospital-is-covered-up/

O'Connor, A. (2006). *Raymond Williams.* New York, NY: Rowman & Littlefield.

Ohler, J. (2008). *Digital storytelling in the classroom.* Thousand Oaks, CA: Corwin Press.

Oliver, J. (2014). *Climate change debate. Last Week Tonight with John Oliver (HBO)* [Video file]. Retrieved from https://tinyurl.com/k5uslqx

Omi, M., & Winant, H. (2015). *Racial formation in the United States* (3rd ed.). New York, NY: Routledge.

O'Neill, S. J., Boykoff, M., Niemeyer, S., & Day, S. A. (2013). On the use of imagery for climate change engagement. *Global Environmental Change, 23,* 413–421.

Ong, W. (1995). *Orality and literacy: The technologizing of the word.* London: Routledge.

Oreskes, N., & Conway, E. (2010). *Merchants of doubt: How a handful of scientists obscured the truth on issues from tobacco smoke to global warming.* New York, NY: Bloomsbury Press.

Orlowski, P. (2006). Educating in an era of Orwellian spin: Critical media literacy in the classroom. *Canadian Journal of Education, 29*(1), 176–198.

Padawer, R. (2016, June 28). The humiliating practice of sex-testing female athletes. *The New York Times*. Retrieved from https://www.nytimes.com/2016/07/03/magazine/the-humiliating-practice-of-sex-testing-female-athletes.html

Padilla, M. (2013, Fall). *EDUC 446: Critical media literacy final reflection*. Submitted as a final assignment for the course.

Pandya, J. Z., & Aukerman, M. (2014). A four resources analysis of technology in the CCSS. *Language Arts, 91*(6), 429–435.

Paris, D., & Alim, H. S. (Eds.). (2017). *Culturally sustaining pedagogy: Teaching and learning for justice in a changing world*. New York, NY: Teachers College Press.

Pearce, M., Duara, N., & Yardley, W. (2016, January 28). Oregon activists remain defiant. *Los Angeles Times*, p. A1.

Perera, F. (2016, June 21). The case for a child-centered energy and climate policy. *Environmental Health News*. Retrieved from http://www.environmentalhealthnews.org/ehs/news/2016/june/opinion-the-case-for-a-child-centered-energy-and-climate-policy

Pérez-Tornero, J. M., & Tayie, S. (2012). Introduction. Teacher training in media education: Curriculum and international experiences. *Comunicar, XX*(39), 10–14. Retrieved from http://www.revistacomunicar.com/pdf/comunicar39-en.pdf

Pesemen, P. D., Aronson, J. (Producers), & Orlowski, J. (Director). (2012). *Chasing ice* [Motion Picture]. Submarine Deluxe.

Petroff, A. (2014, October 9). Lego ditches Shell after Arctic oil protests. *CNN Money*. Retrieved from http://tinyurl.com/jfzv27n

Pew Research Center. (2018, May). *Teens, Social Media & Technology 2018*.

Piaget, J. (1974). *The construction of reality in the child*. New York, NY: Random House.

Piketty, T. (2014). *Capital in the twenty-first century* (A. Goldhammer, Trans.). Cambridge, MA: Belknap Press.

Pineda, J. (2014). *The story behind the picture: Using student photography to develop writing*. (Unpublished master's inquiry project). University of California, Los Angeles, CA.

Postman, N. (1985). *Amusing ourselves to death: Public discourse in the age of show business*. New York, NY: Penguin Books.

Prensky, M. (2010). *Teaching digital natives: Partnering for real learning*. Thousand Oaks, CA: Corwin.

Prescott, C. (2018, August 7). Think Confederate monuments are racist? Consider pioneer monuments. *The Conversation*. Retrieved from https://theconversation.com/think-confederate-monuments-are-racist-consider-pioneer-monuments-100571

Rendall, S. (2014). At elite media, 'scientific' racists fit in fine. *Extra! The Magazine of FAIR – The Media Watch Group, 27*(8), 12–13.

Rich, N. (2018, August 1). Losing Earth: The decade we almost stopped climate change. *New York Times Magazine*. Retrieved from https://tinyurl.com/y8dojc43

Rideout, V., Lauricella, A., & Wartella, E. (2011). *Children, media, and race: Media use among white, black, Hispanic, and Asian American children.* Evanston, IL: Center on Media and Human Development School of Communication, Northwestern University.

Robertson, L., & Hughes, J. M. (2011). Investigating pre-service teachers' understandings of critical media literacy. *Language and Literacy, 13*(2), 37–53.

Robins, K., & Webster, F. (2001). *Times of the technoculture.* New York, NY: Routledge.

Rochlin, M. (1995). The language of sex: The heterosexual questionnaire. In E. D. Nelson & B. W. Robinson (Eds.), *Gender in the 1990s: Images, realities, and issues* (pp. 38–39). Toronto: Nelson Canada.

Roose, K. (2018, October 24). Debunking 5 viral images of the migrant caravan: A group of Hondurans heading toward the United States has been the subject of misinformation on social media. *The New York Times.* Retrieved from https://www.nytimes.com/2018/10/24/world/americas/migrant-caravan-fake-images-news.html

Rosane, O. (2018, September 11). BBC issues first climate change reporting guidelines. *EcoWatch.* Retrieved from https://www.ecowatch.com/bbc-climate-change-reporting-guidelines-2603944755.html

Rubin, A. J. (2018, August 5). A miserably hot Europe is fast becoming the norm: Discomforting signs of climate change. *The New York Times* (International Section, p. 6).

Russo, V. (1995). *The celluloid closet: Homosexuality in the movies.* New York, NY: Quality Paperback.

Rutgers. (2014). *Center for American women and politics.* New Brunswick, NJ: Eagleton Institute of Politics. Retrieved from http://www.cawp.rutgers.edu/fast_facts/

Schiller, J., & Tillett, B. (2004). Using digital images with young children: Challenges of integration. *Early Child Development and Care, 174*(4), 401–414.

Schwartz, O. (2018, November 12). You thought fake news was bad? Deep fakes are where truth goes to die. *The Guardian.* Retrieved from https://tinyurl.com/yaattjo2

Sengupta, S. (2018, August 9). 2018 is shaping up to be the fourth-hottest year: Yet we're still not prepared for global warming. *The New York Times.* Retrieved from https://tinyurl.com/ydyvwfye

Shaheen, J. G. (2001). *Reel bad Arabs: How Hollywood vilifies a people.* New York, NY: Olive Branch Press.

Shamburg, C. (2009). *Student-powered podcasting: Teaching for 21st-century literacy.* Washington, DC: International Society for Technology in Education.

Share, J. (2015a). *Media literacy is elementary: Teaching youth to critically read and create media* (2nd ed.). New York, NY: Peter Lang.

Share, J. (2015b). Cameras in classrooms: Photography's pedagogical potential. In D. M. Baylen & A. D'Alba (Eds.), *Essentials of teaching and integrating visual and media literacy: Visualizing learning* (pp. 97–118). New York, NY: Springer.

Singer, P. W., & Brooking, E. T. (2018). *LikeWar: The weaponization of social media.* New York, NY: Houghton Mifflin Harcourt Publishing.

Singleton, G. E., & Linton, C. (2006). *Courageous conversations about race: A field guide for achieving equity in schools.* Thousand Oaks, CA: Corwin.

Smith, S., Choueiti, M., Pieper, K., Case, A., & Choi, A. (2018). Inequality in 1,100 popular films: Examining portrayals of gender, race/ethnicity, LGBT & disability from 2007 to 2017. *Annenberg Inclusion Initiative, USC Annenberg.* Retrieved from https://annenberg.usc.edu/research/aii

Sontag, S. (1990). *On photography.* New York, NY: Doubleday.

Southern Poverty Law Center. (2018, June 4). *SPLC report: More than 1,700 monuments, place names and other symbols honoring the Confederacy remain in public spaces.* Retrieved from https://www.splcenter.org/news/2018/06/04/splc-report-more-1700-monuments-place-names-and-other-symbols-honoring-confederacy-remain

Stager, C. (2017, April 27). Sowing climate doubt among schoolteachers. *New York Times, Op-Ed.* Retrieved from https://www.nytimes.com/2017/04/27/opinion/sowing-climate-doubt-among-schoolteachers.html?emc=eta1&_r=0

Stanford History Education Group. (2016). *Evaluating information: The cornerstone of civic online reasoning.* Executive Summary. Retrieved from https://sheg.stanford.edu/upload/V3LessonPlans/Executive%20Summary%2011.21.16.pdf

Steele, C. M. (2010). *Whistling Vivaldi: How stereotypes affect us and what we can do.* New York, NY: W.W. Norton & Company.

Stoddard, J. (2014). The need for media education in democratic education. *Democracy & Education, 22*(1), 1–8.

Stop Racism. (2013). *Student made video in Alexander Dinh's ninth grade biology class at the Downtown Magnet High School.* Los Angeles, CA.

Stuhlman, L., & Silverblatt, A. (2007). *Media literacy in U.S. institutions of higher education: Survey to explore the depth and breadth of media literacy education* [PowerPoint file]. Retrieved from http://www2.webster.edu/medialiteracy/Media%20Literacy%20Presentation2.ppt

Sue, D. W. (2010). *Microaggressions in everyday life: Race, gender, and sexual orientation.* Hoboken, NJ: John Wiley & Sons.

Sullivan, J. (2011). *PR industry fills vacuum left by shrinking newsrooms.* ProPublica and Columbia Journalism Review. Retrieved from http://www.businessinsider.com/the-pr-industry-is-filling-in-the-gaps-left-by-shrinking-newsrooms-2011-5

Tester, H. (2013, April 3). Miami-Dade police officer arrested after wife ends up in hospital. *CBS Miami* [Online news report]. Retrieved from https://miami.cbslocal.com/video/category/spoken-word-wfortv/3645558-miami-dade-police-officer-arrested-after-wife-ends-up-in-hospital/

Tiede, J., Grafe, S., & Hobbs, R. (2015). Pedagogical media competencies of preservice teachers in Germany and the United States: A comparative analysis of theory and practice. *Peabody Journal of Education, 90*(4), 533–545.

Tornero, J. M., & Varias, T. (2010). *Media literacy and new humanism.* Moscow, Russian Federation: UNESCO. Retrieved from http://tinyurl.com/j4nrtve

Túchez-Ortega, M. (2017). *Developing literacy skills through lessons of environmental justice* (Unpublished master's inquiry project). University of California, Los Angeles, CA.

Turkle, S. (2011). *Alone together: Why we expect more from technology and less from each other.* New York, NY: Basic Books.

Turkle, S. (2015). *Reclaiming conversation: The power of talk in a digital age.* New York, NY: Penguin Press.

United States Department of Education. (2014). *Expansive survey of America's public schools reveals troubling racial disparities: Lack of access to pre-school, greater suspensions cited.* Retrieved from https://www.ed.gov/news/press-releases/expansive-survey-americas-public-schools-reveals-troubling-racial-disparities

United Nations Educational, Scientific, and Cultural Organization (UNESCO). (2014). Retrieved from http://en.unesco.org/about-us/introducing-unesco

Valencia, R. R. (Ed.). (1997). *The evolution of deficit thinking: Educational thought and practice.* Bristol, PA: The Falmer Press.

Valencia, R., & Solórzano, D. (2004). Today's deficit thinking about the education of minority students. In O. Santa Ana (Ed.), *Tongue-Tied: The lives of multilingual children in public education* (pp. 124–133). Lanham, MD: Rowman & Littlefield.

Vasquez, V. (2003). *Getting beyond "I like the book": Creating space for critical literacy in K-6 classrooms.* Newark, DE: International Reading Association.

Vasquez, V. (2014). *Negotiating critical literacies with young children.* New York, NY: Routledge.

Vega, T. (2014, August 12). Shooting spurs hashtag effort on stereotypes. *The New York Times.* Retrieved from http://www.nytimes.com/2014/08/13/us/if-they-gunned-me-down-protest-on-twitter.html

Vernon, P. (2018, October 23). Caravan coverage plays into Trump's hands. *Columbia Journalism Review.* Retrieved from https://www.cjr.org/the_media_today/caravan-trump-immigration.php

Vygotksy, L. S. (1978). *Mind in society: The development of higher psychological processes.* Cambridge, MA: Harvard University Press.

Wade, N. (2014). *A troublesome inheritance: Genes, race and human history.* New York, NY: Penguin Press.

Westheimer, J., & Kahne, J. (2004). Educating the 'good' citizen: Political choices and pedagogical goals. *PS: Political Science and Politics, 37*(2), 241–247.

Whitman, J. Q. (2017). *Hitler's American model: The United States and the making of Nazi race law.* Princeton, NJ: Princeton University Press.

Wigginton, E. (Ed.). (1972). *The foxfire book.* Garden City, NY: Anchor Books.

Wigginton, E. (1991). *Foxfire: 25 years: A celebration of our first quarter century.* New York, NY: Anchor Books.

Williams, R. (2009). *Marxism and literature.* New York, NY: Oxford University Press.

Wilson, C. (2012). Media and information literacy: Pedagogy and possibilities. *Comunicar, XX*(39), 15–22. Retrieved from http://www.revistacomunicar.com/pdf/comunicar39-en.pdf

Wilson, C., & Duncan, B. (2009). Implementing mandates in media education: The Ontario experience. *Comunicar, 32*(XVI), 127–140.

Wolf, M. (2018). *Reader, come home: The reading brain in a digital world.* New York, NY: HarperCollins Publishers.

Zabel, I. H. H., Duggan-Haas, D., & Ross, R. M. (Eds.). (2017). *The teacher-friendly guide to climate change.* Ithaca, NY: Paleontological Research Institute. Retrieved from https://tinyurl.com/y7jmg3mq

Zinn, H. (2005). *Howard Zinn on democratic education.* Boulder, CO: Paradigm Publishers.

Zuckerberg, D. (2018). *Not all dead white men: Classics and misogyny in the digital age.* Cambridge, MA: Harvard University Press.

Resources

http://guides.library.ucla.edu/educ466

This website hosted by Young Research Library at the University of California, Los Angeles (UCLA) provides articles, movies, photographs, podcasts, lesson plans, websites, online applications, and an array of resources to support critical media literacy research and practice.

Index

Printed in the United States
By Bookmasters